Praise for *Tutor in a Book*

"Finally, an easy-to-read book about study and test-taking strategies! Passionate and caring educators Alexandra Mayzler and Ana McGann have taken knowledge gleaned over many years of working with struggling students and created a valuable road map. Each chapter communicates information clearly and provides systems, worksheets, and achievable strategies so students can take charge and become organized self-advocates. This volume should be part of every student's toolkit and a necessary addition to the family library."

—Susan J. Schwartz, MA Ed; Clinical Director, Institute for Learning and Academic Achievement, NYU Child Study Center; Clinical Assistant Professor of Psychiatry, NYU School of Medicine

"Do your children need help with their school work? Have your efforts to assist them ended in fights and confusion—and no improvement in grades? Alexandra Mayzler and Ana McGann have many years of combined experience in tutoring children. *Tutor in a Book* will give parents a clear road map for understanding their children's learning styles and suggestions for providing them with effective support. I recommend this practical book to any parent who wants to help their child do better in school."

—Michael Thompson, PhD; Coauthor of *Raising Cain: Protecting the Emotional Life of Boys*

Praise for *Tutor in a Book*

"A book your child will come back to time and again for in-depth understanding of class material, methods for writing papers, and techniques for test taking. This practical guide is chock full of worksheets, tips, and strategies to help students achieve academic success. *Tutor in a Book* should be on every child's bookshelf."

—Donna Goldberg, Author of *The Organized Student*

"*Tutor in a Book* is a concise, user-friendly guide that takes tutoring to a new level. Alexandra Mayzler and Ana McGann lay out an easy-to-follow, practical program for helping students learn a new and improved way."

—Jenifer Fox, Author of *Your Child's Strengths*

"Written in a relaxed and easy-to-understand style, *Tutor in a Book* can help students and their parents work together to improve skills needed for success in school. Providing lots of checklists and worksheets, the authors address issues such as learning style, organization, and study skills in a user-friendly, step-by-step format. It's almost like they are there sitting beside you, leading you on to do your best."

—Patricia O. Quinn, MD; Director, Center
for Girls and Women with ADHD

TUTOR
IN A
BOOK

BETTER GRADES
AS EASY AS 1-2-3

ORGANIZATION • TIME MANAGEMENT • STUDY SKILLS

Alexandra Mayzler
Founder of Thinking Caps Tutoring
and Ana McGann

Avon, Massachusetts

For our moms, Faina and Young Sook,
for showing us the why of studying by living it.
(p.s. We finally [might] be able to admit it: You were right. Thank you.)

Published by
Adams Media, a division of F+W Media, Inc.
57 Littlefield Street, Avon, MA 02322. U.S.A.
www.adamsmedia.com

ISBN 10: 1-4405-0214-5
ISBN 13: 978-1-4405-0214-9
eISBN 10: 1-4405-0726-0
eISBN 13: 978-1-4405-0726-7

Printed in the United States of America.

10   9   8   7   6   5   4   3   2   1

Library of Congress Cataloging-in-Publication Data
is available from the publisher.

This publication is designed to provide accurate and authoritative information with regard to the subject matter covered. It is sold with the understanding that the publisher is not engaged in rendering legal, accounting,
or other professional advice. If legal advice or other expert assistance is
required, the services of a competent professional person should be sought.
—From a *Declaration of Principles* jointly adopted by
a Committee of the American Bar Association and
a Committee of Publishers and Associations

Many of the designations used by manufacturers and sellers to distinguish
their product are claimed as trademarks. Where those designations appear
in this book and Adams Media was aware of a trademark claim, the designations have been printed with initial capital letters.

This book is available at quantity discounts for bulk purchases.
For information, please call 1-800-289-0963.

Contents

Part IV: Test-Taking Tips and Tricks—Ways to Ace the Exam

Part V: Emergency Plan—Remember: It's NEVER Too Late!

Acknowledgments

We are deeply indebted to Sara Nelson, without whose guidance and support this book would be but a glimmer of a thought. Sara's confidence in our work and in this project was a necessary ingredient in creating the final product. Thank you to Wendy Simard and Paula Munier from Adams Media for all of your help.

Of course, we'd have little to write about if it wasn't for our inspirational students. It has been a pleasure and an honor to work with you. You have taught us at least as much as we hope to have taught you, and since there's always a lot more to learn, we wish you happy studying!

From Alexandra:

My teaching chops are, of course, thanks to the excellent genes that I got from Babushka Anya, Babushka Aza, and Vova—*spacibo*! Who knows where I'd be today if it wasn't for Felice Solomon, guidance counselor extraordinaire, who first planted the teaching seed into my mind. Thanks to Jill Lauren, whose enthusiasm and attention to her students has been a consistent reminder of where I should set my bar. I am incredibly thankful for the educators and families who believed in and encouraged my work with Thinking Caps, and continue to do so.

I wouldn't be as happy (or sane) without the support of my family and friends. First and foremost, I would like to thank my friend and coauthor Ana McGann. She infused this project with her never-ending energy, stupendously study-able ideas, and excellent grammar. To my best friends, Jaclyn, Dina, Rachel, Jess (P.), Fran, Jess (M.), thank you. My second family, the Stockners: You epitomize my belief that friends are family that I get to pick. And most importantly, to my two men: Papa, who does his best to protect me from New York City cockroaches and other life evils, as well as constantly keeping me on my "toes," and Eugene, my bfw/b—it is so great to have you by my side.

From Ana:

I am truly thankful to my dad, Philip J. McGann, for his unending support and encouragement throughout the development of this project—you've always demonstrated that patience and hard work can get you to where you want to be, simply by doing so yourself. I am sincerely indebted to those gifted teachers whose understanding and patience helped inform and shape the student I am proud to have become, especially Bob Tupper, Liz Zucker, and Sally Larisch; I hope this work is a testament to how much your intuitive guidance has always meant to me.

I am incredibly grateful to my sister, Christina, for continually showing me how teaching can motivate real change in the world—you are extraordinarily and innately talented at everything you do, and it's been a joy to watch you grow to be an exceptionally natural and inspirational teacher. To all of my girls from Holton and friends from NYU: Thank you for being the best cheerleaders one could hope for.

Finally, and most importantly, I'd like to acknowledge my coauthor: Sash, it's been a long trek, but it is more than worth it. Without your incredible diligence, dedication, and timeliness, who knows when or if we would have made it here . . . and of course, as usual, we have definitely learned a thing or two along the way.

Introduction

School. We've been there, done it, and likely will be involved with it in some form or other (as students, tutors, or otherwise) for the rest of our lives. We, Alexandra and Ana, met (at school) in the NYU General Chemistry I Laboratory, where we attempted to not blow up the lab or ourselves while learning something worth waking up for at 8 A.M. every Saturday morning. We each had our own study approaches for this class, but gradually realized that by putting together our methods, we might actually come up with a practical, non-panic-inducing, and manageable way to complete (that is, pass) this course. After many joint study sessions in our dorm rooms, we started to see results in our grades from our combined efforts. With this dually reinforced approach to studying, we even found ourselves using our pooled techniques when helping and tutoring underclassmen and friends.

We soon realized that many of the students we were coaching weren't just having difficulties understanding the material of a given class: They were actually having trouble with learning the material on a deeper level. We thought about more ways to teach students do-able and stick-able study techniques. Using our personal experiences (and keeping in mind the mistakes we made and corners we tried to cut), we created the Thinking Caps Skills Course to help make studying much easier, more interesting, and actually fun for students. We've helped many students through our methods, and this book is the sum of our experiences and insights that we've collected as both students and tutors, which we continue to expand on: we're always learning.

Why Use This Book at All?

Some of you who have made it this far through our introduction may have already rolled your eyes and thought, "Great. One more preachy 'how to succeed' instructional book . . . like I don't *already* get enough of this from [fill in the blank]." While we completely understand that the last thing you need is yet another source of "authority" telling you what to do, that is precisely our point: We want to help you get to where you tell yourself what to do. We've written this book because we were and are students and tutors who have learned things about ourselves and other students, not from others who know better than us. We aren't your parents, but we do hope to pass on at least one helpful or useful technique to you.

One of our goals in writing this book is to get you thinking about what school honestly and specifically means to you. Each student sees the purpose of school from a unique point of view. We want this book to allow you to most effectively and easily get you to where you want to be, even if that means just making it to the end of another school year. Ultimately, our goal is to coach you on how to not just survive another school year, but guide you to a point where you are able to feel proud of all of your accomplishments and work and have no regrets about "how I could've done better." Both of us have had such thoughts of our own, and even seen some of our students have doubts after a tough school year. We offer this book as a way to guide you through such school challenges without overreaching or exhausting yourself, so that you can achieve all of your goals and still have time to enjoy your non-academic life without any "'if onlys."

For some students the biggest question about schools is, "What is the point of going to school?" As tutors, we frequently hear this attitude expressed as, "I get to hang out with my friends and stuff, but other than that, all I do is sit through boring classes and listen to teachers drone on about things I could care less about." Although it is hard to constantly keep in mind, especially in the moments during the school year when you're bogged down and almost drowning under huge amounts of work, we promise: There truly is a point to school. The aim of your classes is to help you succeed in life, no matter what you do, since your life is much bigger than just being in school. Each student has varying reactions to the mere thought of school, ranging from terror, anxiety, or panic, to joy, elation, and even excitement. We ourselves have experienced this entire spectrum of emotions, first as students slogging through high school and college, then as tutors helping our students. Regardless of how you feel about school right now, we hope that you will develop effective and manageable ways to be a student so that you can really like school (or at least not dread going there every morning).

So, What *Is* the Point?

We focus on three main Tools in this book: Organization, Time Management, and Study Skills. While we present these Tools as distinct and separate chapters, we want to emphasize that these concepts are the basis and foundation for academic success. The ideas and techniques do overlap each other, but can be looked at in different ways. Within each section, you will find pages you can use to practice the suggestions we offer in the chapters. While we hope these pages prove useful to you, our hope is that these first steps and our worksheets will provide you with a template you will personalize, and eventually use as an automatic method in all aspects of your schoolwork.

Older and more experienced students may feel that such exercises are tedious or require extra effort, but these are useful suggestions for anyone, which can only become habits with practice. Also, instead of rushing through last minute preparations, we recommend that you consider your year's goals in the month before school starts. This eases you into a school-oriented mindset before the start of the year, while allowing you to continue enjoying your summer vacation. Last minute preparation cramming doesn't exactly set the most positive tone for the school year, nor does it produce exactly the best results. The end result of your well-planned and organized small victories may pleasantly surprise you.

Introducing Our Fabulous Four

For our final introductory piece, we would like to acquaint you with the students who comprise our group of the Fabulous Four: eighth-grade, Jake; his eleventh grade, older sister, Carolina; Bianca, Jake's friend and classmate; and Natalia, Bianca's younger, fifth-grader sister. We will check in on their stories at different stages of an academic year. Their experiences will show how each of them handles an aspect of their schoolwork, from initial preparation and Organization, to developing and honing Study Skills. You hopefully will recognize them as students you might be in class with, each with his or her specific strengths and weaknesses as a student, as well as extracurricular interests—which may resemble your own. Like you, these students have discovered our book and we'll share stories about their efforts to use the Guide and apply the techniques they find most helpful. Their academic challenges are similar to those you encounter yourself, and hopefully their scholastic experiences, which we relate here, will be helpful in your own academic pursuits.

PART I

GETTING STARTED

A PRIMER FOR PARENTS

The child supplies the power but the parents have to do the steering.

—Benjamin Spock

CHAPTER 1.

Parents as Study Partners

Middle- and high-schoolers face the increasing pressure to succeed academically and socially. We recognize that as a parent, you care significantly about how well your child copes with being in such a dynamic academic environment. Understanding your child's attitude toward school and life, and creating a steady environment and routine for a home or school setting strengthens your ability to "partner-up" with your child in encouraging and supporting her academic pursuits. We certainly do not claim to be the next Dr. Spocks of the educational arena—we offer our observations here as suggestions, based on our experiences working with students and their families, which we hope you find helpful in building a strong academic partnership with your child.

Remember When? Taking a Mental Trip Back to School

Although it may seem like your tween or teen wants to do everything with friends and may be slamming her bedroom door shut more often than she is keeping it open, she does still need your guidance and support. Often when starting to work with a new student, we've found it helpful remember our own emotional and personal state during the teen and tween years. We also recommend this as an effective approach to the parents we work with. Put yourself in your child's shoes and remember how you felt at your child's age about school, yourself, and your life (from a social and extra-curricular context). While some people look back on these years fondly, many of us would prefer not to re-live the awkward years of middle or high school. However, reengaging your own past experiences (especially the ways in which you may have tried to push the envelope academically, socially, and otherwise) will help you relate to your child and will make you appear more relatable in the eyes of your child. By remembering and even sharing your own experiences, you can establish a fundamental understanding that you do know that he is going through a tough time and that you are willing to listen or discuss any difficulties he might be going through, and make it an option for him to turn to you if and when he is ready.

Family Time: Creating Reasonable Structure, Limits, and Expectations

At times, it's difficult to know if or where to set boundaries, particularly when it comes to your child's homework and schooling. When you suggest to your child when or how to schedule or do school work, you're likely to be met with such comments like, "Don't worry, I'll do it later," or, "Stop telling me what to do. You're not the boss of me!" With our students, we try to underscore the idea that we are working together as a team. If you approach your child with this team-minded tone, he is more likely to respond positively to your suggestions.

Along with daily and weekly schedules, a few family rules will help your teenager explore his freedom while learning to grow within guidelines. It is important to have the whole family create mutually agreeable expectations, and to communicate these expectations to your teen. For example, everyone is expected to sit down to dinner at the table at 6:30 P.M. with cell phones off, no exceptions. It is important that these expectations are consistently reinforced so that your teen can develop a steady routine, despite the chaos of middle school or high school. These guidelines extend to academic goals, behavioral expectations, and social boundaries. Consistency in your rules will ensure that your teen knows what is expected of him, and what consequences there are if expectations are not met. He will appreciate being informed and knowing you give him responsibility and accountability, and will be able to establish personal expectations for himself and the world around him. We're sorry to say that the thought, "Maybe Dad was right," doesn't occur until much later.

Begin by creating a structured family routine. Your teen can learn to wisely plan his time and find comfort in knowing that even though each day brings its own challenges, his family and certain routines will always be there. Setting firm, enforced ground rules regarding dinner time, regular homework time, and consistent bed time will create a solid framework upon which you and your child can build. An established structure that your child can easily adapt to and work around will allow him to feel some control over his days, instead of feeling that he has been left out of the loop or that his feelings were not considered. A wall calendar to plan out and inform the family of upcoming events and appointments can also be helpful in keeping everyone in the loop.

Hello, Is Anyone There?
Establishing Open Communication

Within the established general schedule, it's also helpful to set aside "check-in" days and ask that your child come to you regularly with updates on school and extracurricular activities. For example, schedule to sit down for a snack and just chat about what's going on at school. Rather than just questioning her at every meal, setting aside a designated, agreed time and asking her to come to you will encourage her to communicate with you. If your child is reluctant to talk about himself, doing a neutral activity together on a weekly basis, such as walking the dog, can help stimulate conversation. Encourage your child to discuss homework, classes, upcoming tests, friends, and activities. If she has mentioned a particularly difficult class or assignment, then make sure to follow up. It is also important that these "check ins" are judgment-free. If your daughter feels you are being critical, she will be less likely to come to you when she is struggling. This can also help avoid the emotionally charged reaction of, "Mom, you just don't get it!"

Allowing her to test her independence doesn't mean that she won't appreciate having you as a safety net, even though it is likely that she will deny that she still needs her mom or dad. As your child matures, it becomes increasingly important that she take on a part of the responsibility in the decision-making process for her academic career. In order for her to learn and continue to grow, she must be allowed to make mistakes and do things in what might possibly not be the most efficient way.

While it's hard to keep from instinctually catching her from each stumble she makes, it is important to keep in mind that you made it through the various trials of middle and high school, and so will your child. We've found in our own teaching and mentoring experiences that the best way to establish a mutually trusting and respectful relationship (particularly with regard to academic decisions) is to make recommendations based on your knowledge and experiences. Discuss your suggestions in depth with her, and allow her the opportunity to and encourage her to come up with some solutions on her own. In doing so, you show confidence in her intellectual abilities, potential for growth, and capacity to make the right choices for herself, and by extension, enhance her self-confidence.

While emphasizing an approach to learning based on mutual respect for one another, it is also necessary to be realistic about how much your child is willing to share with you. While he might appreciate your asking how he feels about his work in science class, or which teacher or class he enjoys most, it's important to recognize the fact that he may leave out certain facts that have to do with his own behavior and circumstances. For example, you might find out that he dislikes a particular teacher because "she is always picking on me," but fail to mention that this "picking on" is a direct result of his being seated next to his best friend and talking in the middle of lectures or presentations. Keep in mind that you're likely only getting a fraction of the whole story, and refrain from prematurely judging a situation. This also extends to a child's opinions and comments on how she is being graded "unfairly" by a "really tough teacher." Your child is likely to volunteer certain portions of information freely, while knowingly leaving out pieces that complete the whole picture, such as the fact that she forgets to write down the homework assignment for the tough teacher's class.

Conference Calls:
Your Child in a Greater Academic Context

The incredible emphasis on good grades is a very heavy burden for any student to carry, and students can be quite sensitive to receiving a lower-than-expected mark. Talk to your child about what and how she can improve in classes, rather than focusing on blame for what has already happened.

As the school year progresses, be aware of the challenges your daughter may be facing. Does she seem to be struggling with math class? Is she having trouble with a particular teacher? Is she constantly arguing with a group of friends? If your daughter's behavior has changed or you start to see dips in her confidence or performance, make sure to recognize and work toward a solution that the whole family has a part in. Let her know that you aren't only interested in hearing about the good, but that you're also available to help her or find others who can provide support. Many times, arguments and miscommunication occur over poor grades because of frustration and fear.

A productive conversation with your child focuses on asking how she feels about receiving the grade, how or why she might have received it (with you filtering out the opinionated statements regarding "harsh graders"), what and how she wants to improve, and finally concluding with how you might be able to help. Avoid questions about how your child ended up with such a low grade because these questions will likely be met with confrontational and defensive responses. If you would like to establish a relationship with your child's teachers, it is important to talk to your child about it. Though you certainly do not need the permission of your son or daughter to speak with his or her teachers, informing your child of your intentions is helpful so it doesn't feel like you are going "behind his back" or "spying on her" just to make sure that he or she is staying on track. He will be more likely to open the lines of communication if he knows that he is part of the dialogue.

Your child also needs to understand the importance of self-advocacy and seeking help. For example, if she is having trouble with a class, point out that she can get help by working with a teacher, tutor, or friend, and if she is struggling with social problems that she can chat with the school guidance counselor, a family friend, or cousin. Let her know that feeling overwhelmed is normal for everyone and that she doesn't have to handle stress alone. Consider the boundaries of your relationship and acknowledge that you may not be able to fix all of your child's problems, but that you can help her seek out support.

Study Buddies: Helping with Schoolwork

Some students are comfortable with asking for help while others are reluctant, as it can be difficult for students to admit to a parent that they are struggling. Encourage a mutual learning environment. For example, consider setting up a study space where you are do your work or reading while your child does his homework. That way, if he has a question, he will be more inclined to ask. When your child does come to you with questions, be flexible and patient in your explanation. It is important to keep in mind that there are different methods of introducing material, especially if your child tells you that you're teaching him the wrong way. Remind your child that just because you learned it a different way, doesn't mean that it is wrong, and ask your child teach it to you his way. Use the resources provided by his teacher and together look through examples. Rather than just teaching or reviewing a concept, discuss with your child how he could find the answer or where he could look to review.

As we'll discuss in detail in the following chapter, each student learns in an individual way depending on his or her strengths and weaknesses. You may find yourself surprised that what you thought was easy in school, your child struggles with, while other topics that you still find difficult to wrap your head around make perfect sense to your child. The way that we learn and the speed at which we are able to learn varies greatly from person to person. An awareness of your own learning tendencies, as well as those of your child, will allow you to recognize when she is overwhelmed or struggling and help you in being a helpful study partner for your child.

CHAPTER 2.

Your Child's Learning Style

Researchers are learning more and more new information about the brain—discoveries occur on a daily basis. While it might seem that most questions about the brain have been addressed, the truth is that we have figured out only a small fraction of the 3-D puzzle that is our brain. In this section, we'll briefly discuss the brain as it is relevant to understanding and identifying learning styles. We have a tendency to be science nerds, but we'll refrain from going into too much detail. However, we believe that a basic comprehension of the brain and its role in how we learn is necessary to identify appropriate learning strategies for each individual student.

Why Our Brains Matter in How We Learn

The human brain can be compared to computer: Its various hardware components have individual and cooperative functions such that the machine executes tasks in a systematic fashion. The cerebral cortex is like the hardware of our brain where the bulk of our information processing takes place. The cortex has two main halves: the right and left hemispheres. We will further explore the processes associated with each region in the next section. In each of these hemispheres, there are distinct areas solely devoted to specific functions (such as language comprehension and visual perception). Certain areas deal only with incoming information about motion, speech, hearing, touch, vision and sound; others just process this information; and still other regions "decide" how to respond to this information.

These assessment-oriented regions control memory, attention, organization, awareness, goal formation, decision-making, abstract thinking, and other "executive functions," acting as the CEO of the brain and body. Information follows a specific route, or pathway, once it is perceived by the brain. The pathways differ from person to person.

A student's strengths are greatly influenced by which hemisphere of the cerebral cortex is dominant and how the two sides of the brain work together. The significance of hemispheric dominance has often been misinterpreted as there are constant changes in the field of brain science. Many people mistakenly believe that the dominant hemisphere of the brain (right or left) solely determines physical aspects of an individual, such as right- or left-handedness. However, studies show that the dominance of a hemisphere has more to do with how a person views, interprets, and experiences the world. While the factors and pathways involved in dominance are not fully understood yet, studies have shown information about how each hemisphere processes information.

The left hemisphere of the brain is thought to deal with the synthesis of information that is logical, analytical, sequential, or empirical in nature, such as perceiving or conceptualizing information from a larger perspective. Examples include determining the location of your keys in relation to the coffee table and the front door, or determining the probability that the teenager driving next to you will run through the stop sign in front of you. People who are "left-brained" tend to process information better by verbally, and have been found to excel in rules and structure of language.

The right hemisphere of the brain is thought to be responsible for creative, intuitive, holistic, and nonsequential thinking. It is the part of our brain that allows us to picture how we want something to look before we put it down on paper. Examples include understanding the detailed functions of a new cell phone, judging the distance you need to clear between steps on a staircase, or being able to orient ourselves when we're lost in a maze.

Although the two hemispheres have distinct characteristics and responsibilities, they are tied together and communicate via complex signals. For example, things that appear on your left are processed by your right hemisphere, while objects on your right are processed by the left hemisphere. The two hemispheres are able to process and produce an understanding or response by communicating with each other through another specific pathway. Almost everything that we do requires the interaction of both sides of our brains to manage and complete given tasks. Additionally, both hemispheres are equally capable of learning (specifically, acquiring and understanding) information, it just happens by different means of processing.

Learning Styles

How the brain takes in and processes information is a crucial component of how we learn. We'll describe in more detail some types of learners in the next section. By understanding which learning tendency your child's brain follows, you will be able to help translate that into more effective and efficient learning methods. Additionally, you may even find that as your child ages or matures, his tendencies may change as well. Depending on your child's learning style, some strategies may work better or worse than others.

Throughout this book, we will suggest various Study Skills that are geared to different types of learners. However, this does not mean that a student should only use one type of study method, and we offer this information on learning tendencies and preferences to help guide your child in adapting his study approaches to his strengths. To help identify the study techniques that are compatible with your child's learning style, we will begin by discussing different types of learners.

Visual Learners

Visual learners, as the name implies, are people who work best by seeing information. For this type of learner, the pathways of the brain are strongest when information is delivered through the eyes. If your child is the type of student who finds that notes on a board or pictures in a textbook help her understand the concepts that she is learning, then she is probably a visual learner. Students who are visual learners benefit from drawing illustrations to go with words and concepts and from connecting concepts with visual images. For example, when studying vocabulary, a visual learner would find it helpful to draw a picture that describes the word. Visual learners should use graphic methods to organize and plan out ideas. By drawing images, the visual learner will best be able to process the information.

Auditory Learners

Auditory learners are individuals who find it easiest to process and remember information if it is spoken out loud. For example, students who prefer to record a lecture and then listen to it several times have strong auditory pathways. Such learners benefit from talking out ideas and concepts, repeating or singing key words and phrases, and discussing topics to process the information fully. Auditory learners should concentrate their efforts on listening and repeating information rather than taking it down on paper.

Kinesthetic Learners

Kinesthetic learners are those who process information best by touching, doing, or physically working through concepts and problems. Your child is likely a kinesthetic learner if he finds it most effective to solve math problems by moving around or physically manipulating objects or easiest to grasp the plot of a book by acting it out. Kinesthetic students work best when they can create physical Associations with concepts. The next time your child is trying to memorize a long list of vocabulary words, don't just suggest that he write out Flashcards. Suggest that he place the Flashcards in different parts of his room and then walk from area to area as he reads out and repeats each word. By relating a word to an action, like walking from one corner of the room to another, your child will increase the likelihood of being able to recall the word and its definition.

Learning Differences

Just as people have different color hair or prefer different flavors of ice cream, people learn in different ways. Individuals with learning differences are capable of accomplishing or succeeding in any given area. Having a learning difference requires that a person use techniques that cater to both weaknesses and strengths alike. Each person learns in a unique way and whether or not your child has a learning difference must be determined by working with a learning specialist and a psychologist or psychiatrist.

What Does the Term "Learning Differences" Actually Mean?

A learning difference (LD) is a way that a person's brain functions that can make it difficult for him to learn in a conventional or cookie-cutter way. This doesn't mean that the brain is

What's Your Learning Style?

In order to figure out the best approach to learning, work with your child to identify her learning type. Together, read the list carefully and check the statements that apply.

Visual Learner

I prefer reading over notes than hearing the information.	
I like to make lists for my goals and assignments.	
I need quiet to be able to study.	
If someone asks me a question on the spot, I need time to figure out the answer.	
I'm comfortable looking at graphs and charts.	
It helps me to draw a picture to remember a word.	
My books, binders, and folders are color coded.	

Auditory Learner

When I'm studying, I like to repeat the information out loud.	
I like to listen to music when I'm doing my homework.	
Even when I may not be looking at a speaker, I comprehend what they are saying.	
I enjoy giving presentations and speaking about topics.	
It is helpful to get quizzed by answering questions verbally.	
When reading is difficult, I read the words under my breath.	
I would rather sit in class and listen to the teacher than take notes.	

Kinesthetic Learner

When I'm studying, it helps to have something in my hand to play with.	
I memorize best by writing things out and making models.	
I enjoy acting out information (like performing on stage).	
I use my fingers to count.	
I need to take frequent breaks when I'm studying.	
I like science lab because I can remember best when I've done something.	
When I read, I keep track of my place by moving my finger across the page.	

malfunctioning; it just means that the pathways that the brain uses are unique to that person. These differences can be expressed in various ways, and individuals with LD might find particular things more difficult to learn than their peers, while also showing strengths in areas that other people typically find quite difficult. This might sound a bit vague, and honestly, it is. The brain is an incredibly complex machine that specialists and professionals spend a lifetime studying without completely understanding.

Learning differences encompass the vast spectrum of how we see, hear, feel, consider, interpret, memorize, and express ourselves. The brain, since it is a very specialized and intricately constructed organ, uses specific areas to receive, process, and respond to a given stimulus. Since researchers, scientists, doctors, and various other professionals have still not discovered nor explained how exactly the brain can operate and control all the things that we do (from breathing to remembering when your dog's birthday is), it's often difficult to figure out when you're dealing with a learning difference and how exactly to go about managing it. We won't go into the detail of a medical textbook, but we'll briefly cover some of the more practical (and relevant) aspects of having a learning difference.

Helping Your Child Learn with LD

As parents, your role is to help your child understand his learning difference and embrace his strengths and weaknesses. Although school work may not be as easy to a student with a learning difference as it is to his best friend, a clear understanding of your child's learning profile will allow him to work with his challenges. If your child has been diagnosed with a learning difference, have a frank conversation with him and help him have a greater awareness of the learning difficulties. It is frustrating for a student when he doesn't understand what is going on with himself. Introduce your child to role models who worked to overcome their learning difficulties, such as Hans Christian Andersen, Alexander Graham Bell, Winston Churchill, Bill Cosby, Tom Cruise, Walt Disney, Magic Johnson, Jay Leno, Henry Ford, Steven Spielberg, Woodrow Wilson, Whoopi Goldberg, and Agatha Christie. If your child remembers that he learns differently and understands how to use his strengths to work with his weakness, he will be able to succeed in and out of the academic environment.

For a child with learning differences, the most important step is helping him find effective learning methods, which may entail adjustments from traditional types of study. Working with a learning difference requires that you and your child be aware of his talents and limitations. You need to be conscious of how to overcome any challenges these aspects may present, and to make sure that your child is receiving the appropriate support he needs to do his best.

Not all academic difficulties are a direct result of a learning difference. However, if you've found that despite your child's best efforts, suggestions to improve her study habits are not effective, it could be beneficial to consult with a learning specialist. In doing so, you will at the least be better able to understand your child as a learner, and even pinpoint areas in which he can foster study techniques that are more effective. Additionally, if your child does struggle with a learning difference, consulting with a learning specialist or psychologist can help her redirect her energy to better tackle any weak areas.

Your child needs access to the specific type of assistance she requires based on her type of learning difference. There are many resources available for students and families, so don't hesitate to ask for them from your school and teach your child to be an advocate for himself. This may mean having your child undergo an initial evaluation to determine exactly what learning difference affects him, how he demonstrates this difference, and what accommodations or assistance he would best benefit from.

Types of LDs

Now that we've talked about learning differences in general terms, we will look more closely at the most common types of LDs.

ADD/ADHD

This particular area of LD has been given a great deal of media attention, which means that there are many misconceptions people may have about it. Some people think ADD means an individual who is totally out of control and bouncing off the walls. However, this is decidedly untrue. While sometimes, ADD/ADHD students have a tendency to be hyperactive or overly energetic, the reality of this learning difference is much more complex. Students with ADD or ADHD may not be able to focus consistently for prolonged periods of time, or they may become too engrossed in a given task and unable to tear themselves away, even if there is other work that must be addressed. Essentially, individuals with ADD/ADHD cannot use their attention appropriately. They may have difficulty starting or stopping assignments, require extra time in completing tasks, and have difficulty processing and/or remembering given information. As a result of their inability to manage their attention effectively, they struggle with having fluency or automaticity in their learning processes.

Dyslexia

Individuals who are dyslexic have difficulty translating written words into understood concepts. This does not mean that they do not comprehend or recognize the concepts that have been written about, but rather that they have trouble with the reading process and the decoding itself. As a result, often those who are dyslexic may struggle with reading directions, multi-step problems, and complex reading passages. To compensate for these challenges, people with dyslexia often demonstrate a greater capacity for memorization.

Executive Functioning

Executive functioning is a term that refers to the mental processes the brain performs to connect previous experiences (including knowledge acquired earlier) with current or immediate actions or decisions. This sounds like an ambiguous umbrella term and it is. Executive functions are hardwired in the neural pathways that are concentrated in the forefront of the brain (frontal lobe), and are among the most difficult and sophisticated brain processes to learn. This includes the conceptualizing and processing of abstract ideas and means of delegating and prioritizing information. Understandably, these are the pathways that are formulated last, only emerging in more advanced stages after the rest of the body and brain have achieved maturity. Executive functioning really develops between the ages of eighteen and twenty-seven.

Executive functions include the abilities to make plans; organize oneself, including one's thoughts, ideas, and actual stuff; awareness and management of time; and the capacity to self-monitor, self-reflect, and self-evaluate. Individuals who deal with learning differences that involve executive functions often have trouble managing their belongings, their time, their thoughts and speech, and may not know when to ask for help. This particular area of learning differences stems from an area of the brain that still is not as well-understood. As a result, it can also be expressed in a variety of other ways than those described here.

Language Processing

Language processing is an area of learning differences that can be expressed as weaknesses in reading comprehension and expression of one's thoughts or emotions. This does not mean that people who experience weaknesses in language processing are incapable of reading or understanding a concept, or experiencing thoughts and making connections in meaningful way. Language processing can hinder a person's ability to fully comprehend a written work, or make it difficult to express ideas. Often, a person who works with language processing issues may find it difficult to find the right words while knowing what he wants to say. Language processing can be compensated for by using techniques that help a student to either understand material on a deeper level, or allow him to move past tiny details to elaborate ideas in an effective manner.

Memory Deficits

This is another large area of learning differences that has yet to be fully investigated, but we'll give a brief overview of here. Typically, memory is separated into two categories: Working (or short-term) memory, and long-term memory. Working memory refers to the capacity to retain and juggle information in an "in the moment" situation. An example (that we do not encourage or endorse, but know is a common occurrence) of using short-term memory is often seen when a student has forgotten to study for a vocabulary quiz in her foreign language class, and hurriedly memorizes the list of words and definitions minutes before the quiz and is stressfully, but successfully able to remember enough information to get through the quiz, promptly forgetting the just-acquired information. Long-term memory refers to the more intricate routes the brain uses to encode information on a deeper level. This would be like being able to recall the order of operations rule in math at any level without having to restudy it: Please Excuse My Dear Aunt Sally. This mneumonic device has been learned and practiced in such great detail that the brain is able to store the concept effectively and sustainably. Individuals who have difficulty with either type of memory can use various strategies to compensate for it. There are also exercises that can supplement these techniques, which should be worked on regularly to achieve an optimal capacity.

We can't tell you whether or not your child works with a learning difference, but we have helped students adjust their study regimes to make their learning habits more effective. We fully recognize the need to individualize a study program for every student, with or without LDs, and here we'll offer some options that many different types of learners have found helpful. To allow any type of study to work you need to recognize that your child has a learning difference and that her learning difference shows itself in specific areas, and she may find that certain sections of this book target her weak areas better than others.

PART II

WHERE ARE YOU AND WHERE DO YOU WANT TO GO?

ASSESSMENT AND GOAL SETTING FOR PARENTS AND STUDENTS

The more that you read, the more things
you will know. The more that you learn,
the more places you'll go.

—Dr. Seuss

CHAPTER 3

Taking Inventory of the Situation Together

Winnie the Pooh knew a few things about himself when he said, "I am a Bear . . . and long words Bother me." It seems to us that he must have taken some time to think about his strengths (like eating honey) and weaknesses (such as long words) to establish this sensible awareness of himself as a bear. If Winnie the Pooh had attended school, he likely would have approached his studies in exactly this way. He would have started with an evaluation of his strong suits and weaker areas so he could set goals. Having grown up hearing Winnie the Pooh stories, we will take a page from his book and begin by understanding and assessing who we are as students.

Where Are You?

In the previous chapter, we discussed different types of learners and the importance of understanding who you are as a learner. Now that you have a good sense of how people learn, we will move on to your current academic situation. In other words, we ask you to ask yourself: How are things actually going? The purpose of this is to first identify the areas that need improvement, and then to decide what steps you will need to take in order to improve. Knowing how you're doing will help you determine whether or not you need to make any changes in how you study, and will also help you set up goals and establish a game plan to achieve these goals. It is a good idea to check on where you are in the course of your game plan every now and then, to make sure that you're still on the right track.

To assess the situation, you might want to think back to comments from your teachers and your school record. Are there specific comments that you heard your teachers make consistently? Suggestions that your parents seemed to repeat on an on-going basis? Did your grades really reflect the amount of work you were doing? Were they what you wanted them to be? In order to help hone in on your "squishier spots," answer the following questionnaire as truthfully as possible, keeping all these things in mind as you read through each statement. This is NOT a test!! There are no "right" answers here, and this questionnaire is just a tool that will help you determine where your strengths and weaknesses lie.

worksheet:
assessing the situation: where am i?

In this questionnaire, we'll review three separate sections of statements. Respond to each using following scale: Always, Never, or Hmm, Kinda. When you have completed each section, tally up the number of each Always, Never, and Hmm, Kinda responses at the bottom in the corresponding blank provided.

Where in the World . . .

I know where my materials are (notebooks, text-books, worksheets, etc.).

I have a system for keeping my stuff in order.

If a friend misses school, I can bring over the assigned homework.

I don't have trouble finding my school supplies when I need them.

My homework is completed each day.

I don't forget to bring lunch/lunch money to school.

I hand in my homework.

My Organizational techniques suit me.

I have all my school materials with me when I'm doing homework.

If I borrow something from a friend, I return it.

I use a planner to keep track of my assignments and upcoming tests.

I remember when I am supposed to do things perfectly.

I think that I'm organized.

If I am confused by a grade on my report card, I can bring all of my tests and graded assignments to my teacher at the end of the term.

I remember where my things are.

When I participate in activities such as sports or other hobbies, I am prepared.

I keep track of when tests and projects are due on a calendar.

TOTAL: **Always**

Never

Hmm, kinda

Minutes, Hours, Days . . .

I have a homework routine that I follow (come home, eat a snack, start my homework, etc.).

I hand in my assignments when they are due.

I am on time to school.

I don't have trouble starting my homework.

I don't have to stay up late to finish my work.

I think I do a good job of managing my time.

I am aware of upcoming tests.

I have lots of time to finish my work.

I don't have to rush to finish tests.

There's enough time in my day to finish everything that I want to do.

When I make plans with friends, I am not the last one to arrive.

My Time Management techniques suit me.

I have time left over at the end of the day to relax.

I feel like I make good use of my time.

When I take a bathroom break during homework time, I come right back to work.

I can follow a schedule that I make for myself.

TOTAL: **Always**

Never

Hmm, kinda

Wait, I Know That!

When my teacher calls on me in class, I can answer the question.

I don't have trouble doing my homework.

When I start studying for a test, I remember hearing about the information in class.

I feel prepared for my tests.

I make an Outline before I start to write.

If my friend is absent from school, I can share my notes from school.

I write a rough draft for a report or essay.

I feel comfortable with my report cards.

When someone in class doesn't understand something, I can help them.

I am not surprised by my test grades.

I understand the reading in my homework.

If I am confused by something, I can refer to my notes.

I don't feel stressed about studying.

I am happy with my test scores.

I tend to remember stuff that I learn.

When I turn over the test, I recognize most of the questions.

TOTAL: **Always**

Never

Hmm, kinda

Your Compass to Figuring Out Where You Are

Now that you've tallied up your responses, it is time to finish creating an understanding of yourself as a student. For each section of "Where in the World," "Minutes, Hours, Days . . . ," and "Wait, I Know That!" if you've tallied more than twelve "Always," then that skill is a strength of yours. If you've added up twelve or more "Never" or "Hmm, kinda," then that is an area that you need to work on. Translate your quiz results into areas of strength and weakness. Remember your key:

"Where in the World," refers to *Organizational skills*
"Minutes, Hours, Days . . . ," refers to *Time Management skills*
"Wait, I Know That!" refers to *Study skills*

Introducing the Study Toolbox

The purpose of this survey was to look at the three areas of the academic processes that make up a student's academic Toolbox and find the strengths and weaknesses of the three components of the study Toolbox. The three sections of the quiz, "Where in the World," "Minutes, Hours, Days . . . ," and "Wait, I Know That!" correspond to the three essential skills of the academic Toolbox: Organization, Time Management, and Maintenance Work and Study Skills. The first section helped determine the strength of Organizational skills; the second measured Time Management skills; and the last section determined how suitable the study methods you use are for your particular learning tendencies. Although we will consider each of the parts of the Toolbox as distinct skills in the following chapters of the book, the concepts and techniques, once you learn them, will combine to form a full academic Toolbox. The goal of adapting and sharpening these skills is to give you the Tools necessary for independent and confident learners.

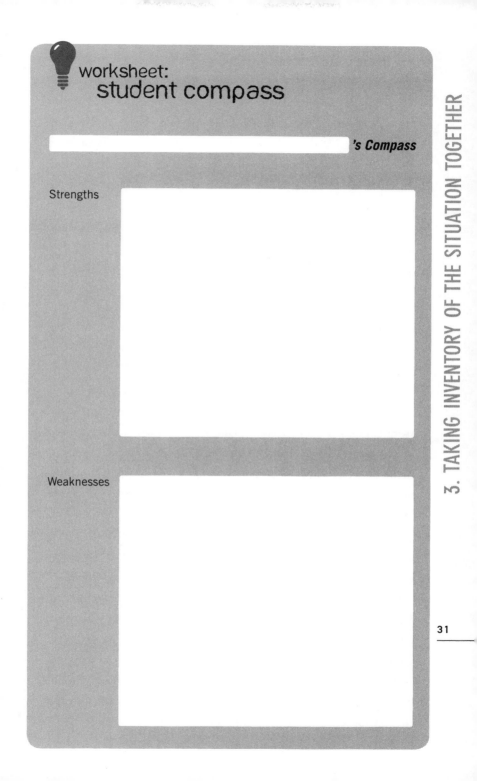

worksheet: student compass

_____ **'s Compass**

Strengths

Weaknesses

Where Do You Want To Go? This Year's Goals

Now that you've figured out where your strengths and weaknesses are, you are ready to think about what you'd like to accomplish or do differently this school year. Maybe after getting your final grades from last year, you promised yourself (or your parents) that this year would be totally different and better; really, you promised! Or maybe you want to get into the next year's honors math class. So, you've decided to do things differently, and that you want to be better, but what exactly do you mean by "better?" Before diving into your school year, you should probably figure out what you want from yourself when it comes to school. In this section, we'll offer a couple of suggestions about how to figure out what's reasonable, and how to stick to your resolutions.

We have also included worksheets that will help you set up both short- and long-term goals you'd like to fulfill for the given year. These worksheets will help you think about what exactly you'd like to accomplish and get out of this school year. These goals range from final grades for each class, to social and extracurricular interests and activities. The purpose of these worksheets and exercises is to help you make these steps part of your routine. You'll find that we're constantly reminding you to practice and repeat what you're learning—the worksheets are just another way for us to remind you.

It's important to set up these goals for yourself so that you constantly feel like you're moving forward through the year, celebrating small victories by completing a plan exactly as you'd set up, and not just going through the motions and getting bored. Set aside some time before the beginning of the school year to set your goals and make a game plan for the year. Instead of waiting to get off track, think about ways you'd like to improve and how to reach your goals, and get everything ready for the new year. You'll be pleasantly surprised about how great it feels to walk into the first day of school fully prepared.

The worksheet on the following pages will help you figure out what you want to accomplish in your upcoming school year. Here are some helpful hints to keep in mind:

1. **Be realistic about your time.** This means being able to recognize the limitations your extracurricular activities will demand of you, including sports practices and games, clubs, instrument lessons, play practices, or volunteer work. Participating in these activities should be part of your personal expectations, since they use a lot of energy and time.

2. **Be honest about academic expectations.** While it is not impossible or unheard of, it is extremely difficult and rare for a student to be able to jump up from a C-level grade to the range of a B+ and above within a short period of time. Aiming too high could just further stress you out and leave you feeling down, when really you may be improving slowly and not recognizing it. Apply the same logic to the Year's Goals/ Objectives and Overall Desired Outcome (which should be a more "big picture" idea of what direction you want to be able to follow on your academic path).

3. **Use all available resources.** If you're unclear about what is truly realistic for you personally, use the best resources possible: your teachers, parents, siblings, tutors, or study buddies (if you have them). Also, having your previous year's report card handy helps in accurately planning what your goals and areas to focus improvement should be.

4. **Be specific.** Define your Year's Goals/Objectives with as many details as possible. For example, if you'd like to concentrate on really knowing all present tense verb conjugations for your French class, which is something you've always had difficulty with (and even received comments on from your teacher), then note in the Goals/Objectives box for your French class: "concentrate on learning verb conjugations."

PART II: ASSESSMENT AND GOAL SETTING

worksheet:
overall goals

Class	Previous Year's Grade	Overall Desired Grade	Year's Goals/Objectives	Overall Desired Outcome/Importance

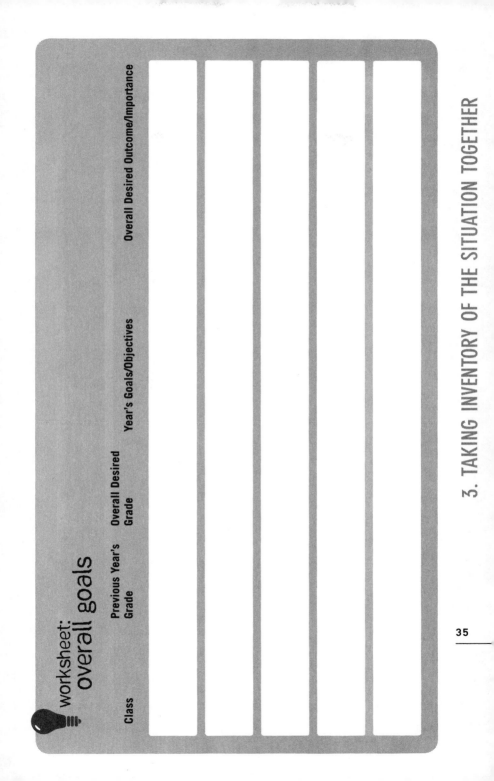

worksheet:
overall goals

Class	Previous Year's Grade	Overall Desired Grade	Year's Goals/Objectives	Overall Desired Outcome/Importance

3. TAKING INVENTORY OF THE SITUATION TOGETHER

meet jake and carolina

Name:	Jake Schwartz
Age:	13
Hometown:	Springfield
Interests:	soccer, guitar, chillaxin with the broz, generally being a bawss
Favorite Music:	anything with a good bass line and beatz
Favorite quotes:	"You can't miss the bear!"

Name:	Carolina Schwartz
Age:	16
Hometown:	Springfield
Interests:	friends, SHS Varsity Soccer, field hockey, tennis, Pirate's Booty and Cheetos, sorting recycling, the beach, reading, SLEEP
Favorite Books:	Welcome to the Monkey House, Much Ado about Nothing, To Kill a Mockingbird, Pride and Prejudice, One Hundred Years of Solitude, The Omnivore's Dilemma, the unending Jordan series
About Me:	"When I was in the sixth grade, I was a finalist in our school spelling bee. It was me against Raj Pattel, and I misspelled, in front of the entire school, the word 'failure.'" (*. . . obviously, ^ = epic fail. <---not in my vocabulary.*)

Jake is a soon-to-be eighth grader, who spent most of his summer at sleep-away camp. He is currently attending a local two-week soccer program with some of his school friends, and ignoring the fact that the school year begins only a week after the program ends. Lately, his mother has been nagging him more and more about how important this upcoming year is and saying that he needs to get his priorities in order. Jake is tired of hearing his mom's blabbering, but he also reluctantly admits the truth of her words to himself. After all, he barely managed to salvage his grades last year after a bad start involving a largely unused planner, lost binders, and last-minute stressful cram sessions for finals.

One day after coming home from soccer camp, he dumps his gear on the floor and notices a sheet of paper perched atop the clutter piled on his desk. Jake moves toward his desk, and with suspicion, reads the following note from his sister: "DO THIS. —C"

Sighing, he turns to the sheet under the note and notices a new book perched atop all of the clutter piled on his desk. He realizes that his mother had "conveniently" repositioned it so he could actually see it, as she'd originally placed it on his once-clear desktop months before for him to look through. Sighing, he picks it up, glances at the book title, and starts to leaf through it. Jake breezes over the intro and beginning pages that discuss the purpose and best ways to use the manual. Flipping past this discussion, he looks at the overall goals worksheet on page 34. After some thought, Jake considers filling in the blank spaces with his classes for the upcoming year. He thinks back to his classes of the previous year, remembering that his math and life science classes were more difficult, while his history and English classes were easy A's, and that he ended up doing all right in Spanish. He continues thinking about his progress, when his nosy, overachieving, know-it-all older sister, Carolina, walks in.

"Oh, I didn't hear you come home . . . you found it." Carolina casually wanders toward Jake's desk to peer over his shoulder, curious to see what her brother is distracted enough by to not yell at her for barging in. "Hey . . . that looks familiar."

Jake raises an eyebrow at his sister, and grumbles, "Yeah. . . . "What do you mean? It's just something I found lying around in my room . . . which reminds me: what are you doing in my room?"

Carolina, ignoring this last comment, says nonchalantly, "Yeah, Mom made me use that book when I was your age. Let's just say, I think it's definitely worth at least some of your attention."

Jake is more than aware that Carolina currently excels in all of her academics. She gets particularly strong grades in math and science, while struggling somewhat with history. Thinking of his sister's difficulties with what has become his favorite subject, Jake smirks to himself. This is one area where things have always been easier for him than for Carolina. However, in further thinking about his sister's seemingly immaterial comments, Jake realizes that Carolina must have learned how to become a stellar student by using the skills introduced in the very book he holds.

Re-energized to get a handle on his grades, Jake reconsiders his previously passing interest in the book he holds, and sits down at his desk to give the current page he'd only haphazardly filled in more serious consideration. He shoves the junk off of his desk and thinks about his academic strengths and weaknesses, especially as demonstrated by last year's grades and teachers' comments. Jake jots down some goals, and when he finishes, sits back to observe his accomplishment with pride. He grins at his work, satisfied, until Carolina says lightly, causing Jake to jump in surprise, "Uhhh, no offense, but do you really think that what you've got is realistic?"

Jake realizes that Carolina has been looking over his shoulder. "What do you mean, 'realistic'? Of course it is," Jake mutters worriedly, looking back down at the page.

Carolina pauses, then says, "Again, no offense, but I've seen your report cards. . . ."

He looks down at what he's written, and hesitates:

worksheet:
overall goals

Class	Previous Year's Grade	Overall Desired Grade	Year's Goals/Objectives	Overall Desired Outcome/Importance
History	A	A+	Get into AP Euro fresh yr	Finish all AP Hx classes
English	A-	A+	Take fresh Honors class	Get into AP English by Junior yr
Spanish	B	A	Get into Honors Spanish	Take AP Spanish Lang by Senior yr
Algebra I	C+	A	Get into Algebra II Honors	Be able to take Calc by Senior yr
Biology	B-	A	Get into Chem Honors	Take AP Bio Junior yr, AP Physics OR Chem Senior yr

meet jake and carolina

"So? What's wrong with what I have?" Jake demands defensively.

"Well, hate to say it, but science and math aren't exactly your strongest suits. I mean, the grades you want to get in history and English seem totally fine with a little extra work on your part, and the Spanish is pretty do-able in the same way, but the science, and especially the math grade right now . . . dude, c'mon."

Annoyed, Jake bursts out, "Look, just because you're super smart in math and science and get straight As in everything doesn't mean you get to make other people feel stupid!"

Carolina, surprised by her brother's touchy response, backs up with her hands held up in surrender, and calmly responds, "Hey, I'm not trying to make you feel stupid. I'm just saying you have a little more trouble with those classes than the others, but you can definitely change that. It just might take a bit more time and work than you think it will." Only somewhat calmer, Jake looks at his "Desired Grades," notes and erases what he's written in for his Spanish, algebra and biology grades, but then hesitates, unsure of what to fill in.

Seeing his confused look, Carolina asks, "What's wrong?"

"Um, I don't really know what's 'realistic' for me."

"Well, think about how you ended up last year in these classes, and figure out how much effort and time you want to devote to which classes. I mean, I think you have the potential to pull up all three grades a lot, but it depends on how much you're willing to work."

"So how do you manage to get As in all of your classes, even in history, which I know you're bad at?" Jake snickers, but Carolina sighs and says, "Awesome, thanks. It actually took me a while to get to where I am. I mean, there was a point where my grades looked a whole lot like yours did from last year. I had As in science and math, of course, but my history grade was pretty bad, and my French and English grades were shaky at best."

With disbelief, Jake snorts, "Hah. I find that hard to believe, since you're Captain Know-It-All now . . . sooo . . . how shaky was 'shaky'?"

"Hmm. This info does not leave this room or you will mysteriously lose your entire video game collection. In eighth grade, I only managed an A– in math, and a B in earth science. But I also got a low B in English, and only got a B– in French, and finally a spectacular C in history. Yeah, I know, don't look at me like that. It took some serious thought, trial and error, and lots of practice to figure out how exactly to fix my problem areas. It's lucky that you're giving this some thought before school starts. Be as realistic with yourself as possible. If you want, I can help you out."

Jake sighs dramatically, but gives in to his sister's offer, secretly grateful. He has always had a knack for school, and since he could get away with pretty much doing the bare minimum of homework and cramming, he managed to come away each year with acceptable grades. However, Jake realizes that he really does want to do well this year, instead of just getting by as usual, and not just because it would mean getting his mom to ease up on her constant nagging about his studies. He could really show himself, and his parents and teachers too, just how well he really could do.

Jake and Carolina start to revise his goals by discussing his previous year's grades, and decide that, since he'd received a B in Spanish the previous year, Jake would be likely (and able) to improve to the B+/A– range this year with moderate and consistent work, with the potential to move up even higher in future years. They look at last year's C+ in pre-algebra and B– in earth science the same way, planning that Jake could make a moderate improvement then build on it in later years.

"You know, I think I can actually do this," Jake finally murmurs confidentially.

"Well, yeah. You're a smart kid. But there's still one other thing to consider. . . ." Jake looks up at Carolina, caught off-guard by the unexpected compliment. "Yeah?"

"The plans you're making sound great, but you haven't thought about the other activities you do. Don't you have sports and after-school stuff to do?"

"Oh, yeah! I'm doing travel soccer and track in the fall, indoor soccer this winter, and Mom is making me do an extra math class after school. Spring is school soccer, and I think I want to try fencing too."

"Exactly."

"'Exactly,' what?"

"You're taking on too much—think about the plan we just made, and add in all that other stuff. You won't be able to focus only on the school stuff. Don't even start with the whole, 'I'm going to be a professional soccer player' thing because you know that still means you have a better chance of being recruited from a college than just straight out of high school."

Jake pauses, unsure of how to respond.

"If you do two activities each season, there's no way you can also focus on your school work. You've got to think about what you want and what's important to you, and be willing to scrap the rest. There's no point to being a 'Jack of all trades and master of none'."

"Whatever."

Carolina eventually leaves Jake to complete his work on his own. He sits back after filling out his goals more realistically and looks at his it with a satisfied grin. He glances at the clock, and sees that the whole process, after agreeing to collaborate with Carolina, only took him about fifteen minutes, and that he's still got plenty of time to call his friends for a pick-up game of soccer before dinner.

worksheet: overall goals

Class	Previous Year's Grade	Overall Desired Grade	Year's Goals/Objectives	Overall Desired Outcome/Importance
History	A	A+	Get into AP Euro soph yr	Finish all AP History H(x??) classes
English 8	A-	A+	Get into frosh Honors class	Get into AP English by Junior yr
Spanish IA	B	A-	Get into Honors Spanish II	Take AP Spanish Lang by Senior yr
Algebra I	C+	B	Get into Algebra II Honors	Be able to take Calc by Senior yr
Life Science	B-	B	Get into Chem Honors	Take AP Bio Junior yr, AP Physics OR Chem Senior yr

meet jake and carolina

Making a Game Plan: How to Get to Where You Want to Be

Now that your goals are in place, let's get to work on your game plan to meet these goals. You've figured out where you stand, based on your responses to the questionnaire and how your totals align with the Compass. You've either found that you're having a tough time with specific areas of your study habits, or that you've got a basic grasp of each tool, but need to sharpen up. You determined what your academic goals are, focusing on one aspect of your study habits or addressing all three Tools at various levels.

If you've found that one tool is particularly challenging for you, then your game plan will be concentrated on improving this area. For example, maybe you're getting grades that you're happy with, but feel like you're spending all of your time doing work. If this is the case, see the corresponding chapter as follows: for the "Where in the World" section, refer to our chapter on Organization; for the "Minutes, Hours, Days . . ." section, flip to our chapter on Time Management; and finally, for the "Wait, I Know That!" part, see our chapter on Study Skills. Within each of these chapters, we address particular goals and strategies that target your "trouble tool."

However, if you're feeling uncertain or sense that there is a combination of challenges as reflected by the number of "Kindas" and "Nevers" tallied for all three sections, is important to think about where you are in the course of your school year. In the section that follows, we will outline four scenarios that target specific points in the school year. For each, there is a recommended course of action to follow. We all have our strengths and weaknesses, and now that you've identified your trouble spots, you can begin to make headway to change your study habits.

PART III

STUDYING MADE EASY

SKILLS FOR STUDENTS

Everything should be made as simple as possible,
but not simpler.

—Albert Einstein

CHAPTER 4

Organization: Getting Your Ducks in a Row

Have you ever spent more time looking for your homework than actually completing an assignment? Maybe you sometimes have that nagging feeling that you're forgetting something, then walked into class only to realize that your completed homework is still sitting in the printer at home. If any of these experiences are familiar to you, then you'll know that good organization of your materials is an important component of a successful year. Students often start off the year knowing exactly where every sheet of paper is, but gradually lose track of things, even after only a few weeks into the term. So, while we'll start out by talking about being organized in terms of figuring out a system that works for you, it is equally important that you maintain and keep track of your system of choice.

Choosing an Organization System That Works for You

Organization begins with figuring out what type of Organizational System you will use and which materials you will need for this system. Walking into a school supply store can be an overwhelming shopping experience. Binders, folders, paper, and pencils of all shapes, colors, and sizes bombard you from every corner. Run? No!! Before you even leave your room, decide on a system that best suits your personal habits. As an example, the following chart demonstrates two main Organization systems that have been effective for many students.

Organization Systems		
	Binder System	Notebook-Folder System
System works better for:	Those who tend to forget or misplace items such as notebooks, folders, or both	Those who tend to lose individual sheets
Organizational preference:	Those who prefer to keep track of sub-sections and materials all in one place	Those who prefer to keep continuous class/ homework notes separate from handouts

As always, it's important to recognize your tendencies, whether strengths or weaknesses, in choosing a system that works for you. It's a good idea to tailor the system to your personal preferences. For example, if you would rather keep a separate folder within a binder to separate homework work from tests and quizzes, it is important to keep that in mind when shopping for your supplies. However, no matter what system you choose, there are certain essential items that you must include. These items include: a monthly planner divided by week; designated notebooks to be used for daily Maintenance Work in each subject, a technique we will go into depth in Chapter 7; and the pencils, pens, and calculator of your choice.

Once you've decided on a system, make a list (or use ours), and without fear head to the nearest school supply store, where the toughest decision you'll encounter is deciding on a color scheme.

Supplies for the Organization Systems

Binder System	Notebook System
❑ Three-ring binders—one for each subject	❑ Notebooks—different color for each subject
❑ Dividers with labels	❑ Labels for the notebook covers
❑ Reinforced loose-leaf paper	❑ Folders—matching color to corresponding subject
❑ Three-ring hole punch	❑ Labels for the folders
❑ Reinforcements	❑ Tape, in case folders rip
	❑ Three-ring binder—used to house handouts instead of folders
	❑ Dividers with labels

General Supplies:

» Planner/agenda book, desk or wall calendar

» Pencil Case, pencils, pens, erasers

» Index cards and holder

» Highlighter

» Calculator, ruler, protractor

» Post-its/page markers

» Graph paper

» USB drive

» Corkboard/thumbtacks, magnetic board/magnets, dry-erase board/markers

Tailoring Your Organization System

Now that you've have your supplies in hand, let's turn our attention to organizing the system you chose. Regardless of the system, you should have a single transportation folder for dual purposes. Instead of simply stuffing your papers into your bag, your transportation folder should have separately labeled sides for clear

Organization: one side labeled "To Home" for carrying handouts home, and the other side section labeled "To School" for bringing completed homework assignments to school. We recommend splurging on a plastic folder (vs. paper), so that instead of disintegrating at the first hint of rain, your folder will actually make it through to the end of the year.

Binder System

If you've chosen the binder system, you should plan to have a separate binder for every subject. Using dividers, you can create and label sections, "Notes," "Tests," "Homework/Handouts," and "Daily Maintenance Work." Fill the "Notes" section with plenty of loose-leaf paper so that you are always prepared for taking detailed class notes to prepare for tests. The "Tests" and "Handouts" section should be filed whenever you receive those materials. As you receive papers from your teachers, place these in the "To Home" section of your transportation folder and then when you're at home, place the sheets into the right sections in chronological order. You will use the "Daily Maintenance Work" section of your binder to manage any review sheets you receive (we will revisit this topic in Chapter 7 of this book).

For those of you who find that you misplace a great number of things, or would just rather keep all of your belongings in one place, we recommend using a three-inch zippered binder. This ensures that not only are all of your things stored together, but also that all of the binder's contents are secure (there's little chance of anything falling out). In order to organize this binder, make sure that each subject is easily recognizable as being separate from another by using larger dividers, and divide each subject as you would normally (or as we mentioned in the first paragraph: notes, homework/handouts, tests, and Daily Maintenance Work).

Notebook System

Like the binder system, the notebook system begins with an individual notebook for each subject. We suggest purchasing notebooks with nonperforated pages, as these seem to stay in better shape and are less likely to fall out. The notebook system requires additional materials for keeping track of loose papers. You could choose to have folders to carry tests and handouts or maintain a notebook that has folders built into it.

However, since separate folders can be hard to carry, you might rather use a single binder for loose sheets. A great approach is to divide this binder into sections for your various subjects and use each section to hold the appropriate tests and handouts. Another option is the accordion folder, which allows you to keep papers in one place, but does not require punching holes. If you aren't very good about filing your materials, you may find that the binder will work best in the long term. You should have a transportation folder that will be used for bringing homework assignments to school and handouts home for Organization, just as you would with the binder system. This method will allow you to combine aspects of the notebook and binder systems.

Finally, you'll need to keep a notebook titled "Daily Maintenance Work" (or DMW for short) daily maintenance notebook for use especially at home. This notebook can have particular sections devoted to each subject, containing the daily Maintenance Work for the subject—again, we'll come back to the issue of daily Maintenance Work in Chapter 7.

worksheet:
organization system
selection

What to do: Select the Organizational System that works best for you. Once you feel comfortable with the approach, you can purchase the necessary materials.

Step 1: Pick a system that works best for you based on this chart:

	Binder System	Notebook-Folder System
System works better for:	Those who tend to forget or misplace items such as notebooks, folders, or both	Those who tend to lose individual sheets
Organizational preference	Those who prefer to keep track of sub-sections and materials all in one place	Those who prefer to keep continuous class/homework notes separate from handouts

Step 2: Now that you've got your system, take our list on your shopping expedition.

Binder System	Notebook System
❏ Three-ring binders—one for each subject	❏ Notebooks—different color for each subject
❏ Dividers with labels	❏ Labels for the notebook covers
❏ Reinforced loose-leaf paper	❏ Folders—matching color to corresponding subject
❏ Three-ring hole punch	❏ Labels for the folders
❏ Reinforcements	❏ Tape, in case folders rip
	❏ Three-ring binder—used to house handouts instead of folders
	❏ Dividers with labels

Organizing Your Work Space

Having an organized work space is another key to keeping track of exactly where your stuff is. This means keeping your desk and the surrounding area clear of clutter and distracting objects. Many students find it helpful to keep binders on their desks to prevent loose papers from getting stepped on or lost. Also, one of the biggest enemies of productive studying is the presence of a TV or video game set-up. You might find it comforting and even helpful to listen to "study music," and in moderation this is fine, since it can help you focus and block out background distractions. However, TV or video games are actual distractions. We have yet to hear a truly convincing argument about the possibility of correctly solving math problems while watching TV. Also, your computer should be used specifically to complete assignments during your designated homework time. It's unproductive to be instant messaging while attempting to do your homework. Keep your chatting for your down time, when you take a break or wrap up your work. Your workspace should also have a large, visible calendar where you record important dates, such as tests.

Setting yourself up with the right Organizational system doesn't mean you're done. Next, we recommend you adopt our mantra: Constant vigilance! This means a daily, or at least weekly, upkeep of all relevant materials. For example, if you happen to be absent from school, you need to get the class work and file it accordingly. Similarly, if you had to rush out of class and ended up stuffing some papers into your bag, make sure you replace the materials in the proper order that you established in the beginning of the year. You should also set aside one day a week, typically a weekend, depending on when you have time to sit down, to thoroughly check through your notes and papers and make sure that everything is in order. It is important to keep all papers in a specific order and all should be labeled, dated, and in chronological order.

meet natalia and bianca

Name:	Natalia "Nat" Reyes–Jenkins
Age:	11
Hometown:	Springfield
Activities:	dancing, singing, theater, voice, hanging out with friends, SHOPPING!!!!
Interests:	Broadway. Music IS my life.
Favorite Movies:	Cabaret, Music and Lyrics, Wicked!! (i know it's a show, whatever, it totally should be a movie anyways ;P), Prom Night, Get Smart

Name:	Bianca Reyes–Jenkins
Age:	12
Hometown:	Springfield
Interests:	Hanging out with friends, soccer, snowboarding, photography, shopping
Member of:	SMS girls soccer ♥, 10,000,000 Strong for our Troops!, Six Degrees, Student Faculty Government, Cookie Dough = LIFE!!!
Favorite quotes:	"The steeper the mountain, the harder the climb, the better the view from the finishing line."

Natalia snatches up her cell phone at the personalized ring tone of an incoming message, and reads the text from Ashley, "ready? we're on our way." She snags her jacket and heads for the door, grabbing her cell and wallet as she hurries from her room down the hall to the front door, when she collides with her sister, Bianca, who has just returned home after a long afternoon of soccer practice.

"Ow! Jeez, where's the fire?" Bianca grumbles and grabs her right foot, as Nat looks sheepishly down at the mess of things that she caused Bianca to drop on her foot. Scrambling to help Bianca gather her gear and school books from the floor, Nat apologizes in a winded voice, "Sorry, Ash is here, I didn't see you, we're going shopping. . . ." Straightening up, Nat hands her older sister back her now jumbled belongings, and glances at the front door and sees Ashley's mom's car turn the corner to pull up in front of her house.

After yelling a quick, "Bye!" to her mom and sister, Natalia runs to the car and hops in next to Ash, and the two grin at each other at the prospect of a shopping trip, even if it's just to get school supplies. Since her parents had insisted on discussing exactly what she would be allowed to buy, Nat fishes the list that the three of them had finally made together out of her jeans pocket. Glancing down at the list, she thinks back briefly to the conversation at dinner the previous night, when her parents insisted that the family discuss middle school and the changes that they expected to see this year. They even brought out Nat's previous year's final report card to refer to her "tendency throughout the year to misplace her work," commenting that she probably needed to figure out a better way to organize her school materials.

With some groaning and eye rolling, Nat and her parents gradually worked out a work plan that would begin with today's purchase of several key items, specifically for the purpose of keeping better track of her things. Although she'd agreed to the work plan, Nat still feels that it's most important to channel her energies into preparing for the auditions coming up in early October. She had spent hours over the summer perfecting her voice and dance routine and wasn't about to let anything get in the way of starring in her school's fall production of Grease.

Nat sighs and turns her attention back to her list, when she hears Ash giggle, and looks up to see Ash pulling a similar-looking list from her own bag. The two start to whisper and laugh even more, when in comparing lists, they find similar items. "Mom? Did you talk to Nat's mom about what to get for school?" Ash questions her mother, who amusedly looks at her daughter in the rearview, and answers, "Maybe. Why?"

"Oh, no reason, just wondering," Ash chirps back. Ash's mom shakes her head, smiling at the two girls in the back seat, who continue to laugh and compare their lists, until they realize the car has slowed to prowl the parking lot of their destination. "Ooh! There! Over there, Mom!" Ash points excitedly at an empty spot closer to the entrance of the mall. As her mother guides the car to the designated spot, Ash turns to Nat, and grinning, challenges her with the suggestion: "Race ya."

"Hah! Done deal—first one back to the car has to . . ."

". . . buy everyone ice cream!" proclaims Ash. The girls grin at each other; having grown up literally next door to each other since they were three, each knows the other so well she could finish her counterpart's sentences, and tell you how many freckles the other has on her face. Of course, since they've sat next to each other in class, one would think the BFFs shared one brain. There certainly have been enough times in class when a teacher has mistakenly called on one of them by the other girl's name. Bianca lovingly refers to the pair as the "two-headed monster," to which the girls consistently respond by simultaneously sticking their tongues out at her.

However, once Ash's mom has parked the car and given the okay to disembark, the two race toward the mall entrance, slowing briefly only when Ash's mom shouts to watch where they are going, and that they have one hour before she comes hunting for them! Still laughing and chattering, Ash and Nat leave Ash's mom to her own browsing and dash along the well-known course, navigating around larger groups of high-schoolers and moms overloaded with shopping bags of various back-to-school items. Arriving at the large welcoming entrance to the office supply store, Nat grabs Ash's hand and pauses.

"All right. So, rules are: We each have to start from opposite sides of the store, and first one to get back to the car has to text the other. Ready . . . setgo!"

"Hey! No fair, party foul!" Ash cries, as Nat scurries to the left around a large shopping cart headed toward where they had been standing in the entrance way, and rushes in to the right of the store. As Nat slows to see what her starting aisle contains, she happily finds the aisle chock full of binders, the first item on her list. Having reluctantly and sheepishly recognized her tendency to often misplace important papers (and other pertinent school work) the night before, Nat and her parents decided that using a single binder-notebook system would work best for her. This way she can color-coordinate her subjects, and keep track of all of her papers. On seeing shelves fully stocked with multicolored and themed binders, Nat delightedly starts browsing the three-inch three-ring binders for the perfect fit. After paring her choices down, Nat spends a few more minutes debating whether or not to go with her impulse to get the leopard printed cover, she settles on the Harry Potter-themed binder, featuring Ron (*sigh* so dreamy . . .) at the forefront of the equally attractive cast, as her new school binder. Luckily, it even has front and back pockets, five extra large dividers (each featuring a different HP character), as well as a flap-cover that she can Velcro shut, thus ensuring maximal safekeeping of her schoolwork.

Satisfied with her choice, she refers back to her list and grabs five packs of color-coded dividers to insert into her shiny new binder—she'll decide which color is best suited for a given topic at home. Marching hastily down the next aisle, Nat prudently selects a bright pink pencil case (making sure that it is binder-compatible), a pack of sparkly mechanical #2 pencils, a matching packet of sparkly and multicolored pens, and is scrutinizing white-out options when she is interrupted by a sharp poke in her side. Startled from her reverie, Nat whips her head around to see a wickedly grinning Ash darting toward the binder aisle, carrying what looks to be a nearly full basket of goodies. Squealing, the two girls rush to complete their shopping, hoping to beat the other back to the car for the win.

Breezing down the next few aisles, Nat grabs a matching pink, binder-friendly paper hole-punch, a large packet of loose-leaf paper, and stalls momentarily when forced to choose notebooks for her classes. Realizing that she has no choice but to decide on a color scheme now, Nat designates her new notebooks' subjects speedily: blue for English, purple for Spanish, green for science, a Smiley Miley theme for history (she needs something to perk herself up while sitting in her least favorite class), and hot pink for math. She makes for the shortest checkout line, and luck appears to favor her, since she manages to worm her way to the express lane just in front of a wave of people (including Ash) who have also decided to complete their purchases. She snickers as she receives her neatly bagged purchases from the cashier, as she hears Ash moan from her place in line, "Oh no way, that's not fair! And I have to text my mom too. . . ."

Nat dodges through the mall crowd traffic with ease, and races for the car. Setting her bags down, Nat digs through her pocket for her cell and madly starts punching buttons. Arriving only moments later, a breathless Ash scowls while Nat gloats at her victory, laughing uproariously when Ash's glowering intensifies at the buzz of her cell phone. "Whatever, you only won because I forgot to get a new stapler and had to go back," Ash pouts as Nat flips into a handstand and stalks around Ash in slow circles while taunting her with victory chants.

However, both Nat and Ash jump at hearing a cheerful, "Well played, girls!" Ash's mom emerges from the crowded mall entrance, carrying a bag with the unmistakable colors of their favorite ice cream shop. Seeing both girls' eyes light up, Ash's mom continues, "Now since Nat made it back first, she gets first pick of which sundae she gets." Crowing her victory, Nat greedily claims the bag containing her prize, and tortures Ash further by pointedly pondering each flavor and topping aloud. "C'mon!! This is soooo unfair, stop being so mean," Ash whines as Nat finally decides to go with the cookies 'n' cream sundae, topped with hot fudge and rainbow sprinkles. Nat snorts into her first bite of her sundae as Ash scoffs at the remaining treats.

Content with their prizes, Nat and Ash noisily make their way back, singing loudly along with the radio. When they arrive at her house, Nat turns to grab her things, asking Ash, "You gonna be online later?" Ash rolls her eyes and sighs dramatically, responding, "Of course," and Nat laughs, thanks Ash's mom for the excursion, and runs back to her house, lugging her new school supplies. Natalia giddily returns to her room with two large bags, hits the power button on her computer, and dumps the contents of the bag onto her desk to reassess her decisions about which color notebooks she's assigned to her classes. Satisfied with her choices, she writes the subject label on the front of each notebook in black permanent marker. She puts dividers for each subject labeled "Homework," "Notes," "Handouts," "Miscellaneous," and "Tests/Quizzes" into her new binder behind the larger provided dividers, along with a small chunk of loose-leaf pages. Nat prints out a copy of her schedule for the year and attaches it to the inside of the front of her binder, highlighting each class in the appropriate color corresponding to her notebooks. Once she completes this cycle with all of her subject binders, she places her materials in her new backpack.

Bianca walks by Nat's room and pauses in the doorway, observing her sister meticulously placing her binder and notebooks neatly to the side of her desk, and laughingly says, "Ahh, I remember the days when I used to use a binder like that. Good for you." Natalia glares at her sister and continues to carefully organize her bag. Nat peels the price stickers off of the pencil case, rips open the packets of mechanical pencils, eraser caps, and multicolored pens, and gently places the carefully selected writing utensils in their spotless new case. She thoughtfully places her pencil case in the front of her binder and sighs with satisfaction when she hears the distinct chime of an incoming chat message, and reads,

```
Ash920: yo you theres?
```

Quickly putting her newly organized purchases into her school bag, Nat rapidly types back:

```
ddramaqueen: heyhey . . . you playing with the new
goods?

Ash920: lolz of course! my folders are just so
pretty . . . *sigh*
```

Pausing, Nat wrinkles her forehead at the screen before responding,

```
ddramaqueen: wait, why'd u get folders?

Ash920: oh, cuz i hate lugging binders everywhere
. . . they're superheavy!!

ddramaqueen: ah. well i didn't really get to pick
what i got. my parents told me i had to get a
binder since i always loose stuffs

Ash920: lol yeah you do . . . you remember how you
almost forgot to turn in that huge project because
you couldn't find it anywheres???
```

Nat laughs aloud to herself, and types back, shaking her head,

ddramaqueen: yeahhhhh that wasn't such a good time
. . . ummmm brb, dinner

Ash920: yeah me 2 . . .

ddramaqueen: ueah—wanna come over after? my sister
just got the new issue of Vogue, and she left it
sitting in the kitchen ;)

ddramaqueen: sweet! mos def . . . i'll txt when
i'm omw . . . kk, laters :P

CHAPTER 5

Time Management: Getting It Done, Time Left for Fun

So, what does it mean to "manage your time"? Time Management is likely a term that's been tossed at you by teachers and parents alike, who tend to use this as a blanket phrase for "shape up and get your work done!" While it may be tedious or seem pointless to have to consider these words as actually having real meaning, they are in fact significant and here's our translation: Time Management is how you organize your work and complete it within a set timeframe so that you can actually have a life. You should be able to see what you need to do (homework, quizzes, tests, essays, papers, projects, etc.) from a daily, weekly, monthly, and even yearly viewpoint. Obviously, this is much more easily said than done.

We've all, at one point or another, tried to convince ourselves (or maybe others) that we've got everything under control. However, claiming you've got everything under control is meaningless unless you have a plan to act on. If you plan properly and stick to your schedule, you'll find that you can finish projects in a timely fashion. It definitely does take a lot of effort at first, and you won't always be 100% faithful to your plans. However, if you stick with practicing the Time Management techniques we present here, you'll find these exercises become natural and automatic with time.

Ultimately, practicing these time-management skills will help you learn about your own personal learning habits or tendencies.

Once school has started, it generally takes about two weeks for any student to fully get back into a school-oriented frame of mind from summer vacation mode. After two weeks, you will have figured out the pace of your days and weeks overall: your extra-curricular schedule (including sports, clubs, play practice, music lessons, etc.), dinner, breaks, hygiene, and sleep schedule that make up the routine you establish for yourself. It should also take you about two weeks to set up a homework schedule that best suits your needs, based on your classes and activities. If you compare your previous year's work times to that of this year's, you may find that some subjects are now taking longer than expected or than they did in the past. So when you set up your new study schedule, keep these things in mind. The following worksheets should be used from the start of semester to help set up a weekly or rotating schedule, depending on your school schedules, once the pace of your year is set.

Keeping Track of Your Assignments

You should be able to manage what needs to be done in order to be able to plan out when and how you do it. It is nearly impossible to keep all information about assignments, projects, and tests in your head without forgetting any of it. Therefore, it is essential to write down concise information about all tasks to be performed. It saves you the energy cost of having to juggle all of your assigned work in your head while making sure you don't forget anything.

The hands-down best means of keeping track of assignments and tests is to use an academic planner or agenda book. For those of you who don't like the idea of carrying around another book, there is an alternative method we suggest. You can also use a sheet of paper, on which you write down all of your daily assignments. This sheet should be attached to the folder you use to transport your homework to and from school and switched out for a fresh sheet on a weekly basis. Worksheet: Academic Planner Alternative is ideal for you to use for this purpose. Be sure to file old assignment sheets for future reference; these become especially handy when prepping for tests. Even if your teachers post assignments online and you prefer to just e-mail homework to yourself, you should use a planner of some sort to determine a schedule for your daily homework. Begin your homework session afternoon by copying the assignments into your agenda to plan out how to spend your homework time.

Your agenda book or academic planner should contain information about all daily homework. Additionally, you should create an area in each week's pages where you can write down information about projects and tests. In a planner, you can clearly indicate the area where you will log projects and tests with a highlighter. If you are using our Worksheet: Academic Planner Alternative (see pages 66–67), you'll find that we devoted a specific portion to write down this information. Whatever method you decide on, it's crucial that you write down specific information about the project or exam, especially its due date.

Planning Out Your Time

While you might not have homework in every subject every night of the week, a way of keeping track of what you need to do helps you to gauge your workload. Setting up a structured daily, weekly, and even monthly schedule early in the semester will get you through the school year by allowing you to think about your work in terms of these time frames and plan accordingly so that by the time midterms or finals roll around, you'll have no worries! To help you visualize a concrete homework plan, we've created a homework Organization worksheet that will help you prioritize and organize your work efficiently. We recommend using these sheets consistently for two to three weeks in order to get into the practice of recording your daily assignments. After a few weeks of employing the Worksheet: Homework Organization strategy, you'll be in the habit of assessing your planner at a glance to determine how you will go about completing your assignments.

You should use a copy of Worksheet: Homework Organization for each day of your schedule (see pages 70–71). That is, each sheet should vary slightly and reflect which classes you have the following day. This is especially true for those of you who have a rotating schedule. You will have different sheets with different rankings for Order of Completion for each day of your schedule (e.g., day one, day two, etc.).

When it comes to your daily planning routine, here is our suggestion for a plan of attack:

1. **Review.** Using your agenda book/assignment planner, scan for which assignments are due the following day.
2. **Transcribe.** Rewrite homework from planner to "assignment" column of Sheet 1, which you should post on the wall above your workspace each day.
3. **Number the Subjects in their Order of Completion.** In the boxes in front of the Subject Name column, number your subjects in order of most demanding to least, and fill in the appropriate assignment in the Assignment box. We recommend starting with the most difficult subjects for you, since you'll likely have the most energy and attention to invest at the start of your work session. While you should (and likely will) take breaks periodically during your homework time, you're freshest at the start, so you might as well get the hardest bits out of the way first.

worksheet:
academic planner alternative

When to use it: If you find that using an agenda book is inconvenient, then use this worksheet. However, this is worthless if it becomes just another paper stuffed into your bag.

How to use it: At the beginning of each week (i.e., Sunday evening), staple a copy of the worksheet to your transportation folder, making sure to remove and file away the previous week's sheet.

	Mon	Tues	Wed	Thurs	Fri	Sat	Sun
Math							
English							
Science							

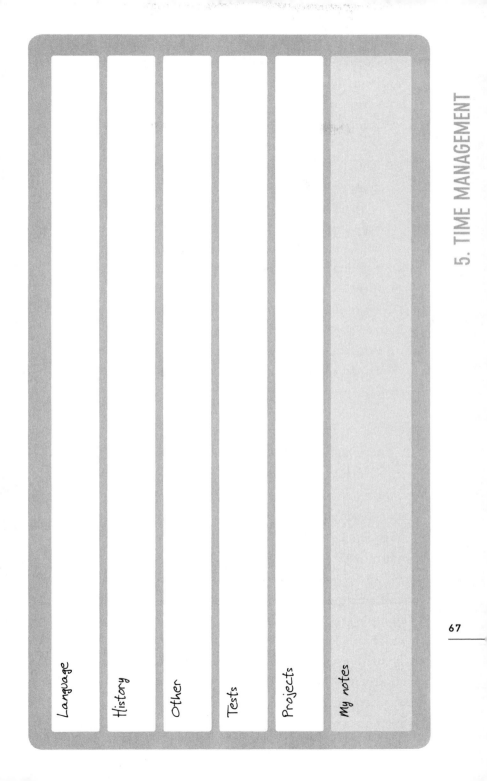

Language

History

Other

Tests

Projects

My notes

4. **Duration.** This is the toughest part—figuring out how much time to devote to each subject. As with many students, you'll find that some subjects are a breeze and take very little time to get through, while others require significantly much more attention, both in terms of time and effort. The estimated time frame devoted to each subject should be flexible and not overly demanding. That is, be realistic about how tough a subject is for you, and base your time estimate on your personal experience.

In planning out your assignments, you need to be aware of your tendencies. That is, if you are a person who must be absolutely correct all of the time, or if you are someone who would prefer to do the bare minimum to just get it done, you need to be able to recognize when these characteristics present themselves in your work and adjust your habits so you can get your work done effectively.

Perfect Is the Enemy of the Good: How to Mediate the Perfectionist

A smart French guy named Voltaire once said, "Perfect is the enemy of the good." It's kind of difficult to figure out what the great philosopher meant, but we will translate it here to mean that perfectionism can get in the way of getting good stuff done. If you find yourself getting penalized for not handing in a draft or homework because you're still busy tweaking your work or maybe you find yourself having difficulty even getting words onto a page because you're overly concerned with choosing exactly the right words, then you may be falling for the "perfect is the enemy of good" trap. Similarly, you might be putting off a make-up quiz, test, essay, etc. because you're worried that you're not quite ready yet. You're not alone. Many students find themselves stuck in these types of situations. Hey, even Superman isn't always one hundred percent on his game, so here are some thoughts on how to get you unstuck and moving forward.

Perfectionism can be a roadblock when you find that you are unable to get stuff done on time! While in certain cases, your insistence on completing tasks flawlessly may be a good thing, there are other times when such nitpicking becomes a problem more than an asset. For example, let's say you have an English essay assigned as homework, but you ignore the interim and final deadlines because you're not quite satisfied with your work. By the time you hand in your drafts and final paper to your teacher, you've been penalized by an entire grade because you finally turned these assignments in three to ten days after the due dates. A similar situation is if you wanted a part in the school musical, but felt too unprepared when your audition time came around, so you backed out completely and deprived yourself of what could have been a challenging and fun experience. These are clear examples of when perfectionism leads to ineffective working habits; you're more likely to get stuck, or not even be able to start a project, just because you're too busy quibbling over tiny, (and for the time being) insignificant details.

Instead, try to be more aware of your tendency to find faults, and focus more on correcting them in the moment. If you find yourself stalling in either starting or working through an assignment, realize that work is a process. You need somewhere to start in order to create a final product you can be happy with, so save the pickiness for the appropriate time and place in your work process. Drafts are just that. They are works-in-progress that you can improve on, but in order to do so, you have to build a foundation on which you can expand. You can't put the roof on a house without first building the house. Sometimes you may need to settle for just getting it done, especially if you're working under deadlines. You may even be tempted to go above and beyond a given

worksheet:
homework organization

Date:

Homework I need to do tonight:

Order of Completion	Subject	Time to Spend	Assignment
	English		
	Social Studies/ History		
	Math		
	Science		
	Other/Foreign Language		

Time when I started my homework:

Time I ended my homework:

I feel that I finished my homework:

Too quickly   *In the right amount of time*   *Too Slowly*

1   2   3   4   5

MY NOTES:

assignment, completing an entire draft when your teacher asked that you hand in an outline. In this case, you may lose points for not doing the job you were assigned, or your work might not be acknowledged at all. Yes, it is a difficult task to accept given your perfectionism, but in some situations, what is expected of you outweighs what you expect of yourself.

Since you know that you tend to overdo your work, how can you prevent yourself from doing so? First, be realistic about your habits; if you accept that you often spend too much time on sections of your work because "they aren't quite right," you should set interim goals for yourself. Figure out what you need to complete and when, and write out a detailed schedule and stick to it! This means that if you know you only have a certain amount of time to finish an assignment, set a timer for yourself, or even better, ask someone (a friend, sibling or parent) to "proctor" your work and tell you when time's up. If you find it tough to find the words to start out with, or are confused about what exactly you are supposed to be answering in response to an assigned question, don't let the blank page or screen get to you. Write down whatever comes to mind, whether it's a formula, equation, or random (but topic-related) words. This start will likely jog your brain further for relevant information, and you will likely find yourself gathering speed and making sense in your notes. If you really feel like you're stuck within your personal deadline, (e.g., you just can't find that perfect word, or you keep getting the wrong answer for this one math problem, etc.), highlight the problem area by circling, underlining, or making a note that you'll come back to it, and move on. Once you've met the set goal as written out on your schedule, put down your pencil, or save and close the file, and get up and walk away without indulging your knee-jerk, "I should really look that over one more time" impulse. You will actually benefit from time away from your work, so that when you come back to it (as planned in your schedule), you will benefit from your break and be more efficient in your Editing, avoiding potential future "Great, I'm stuck" moments.

Don't Be "That Guy"
(the "Just Get It Checked Off" Student) . . .

. . . Or, why checking your work matters! There will be many times when you just don't want to do it: your homework, your preparation for a test, your research for an essay that's assigned, even just writing down those few things you really need to remember to bring to class with you the next day. Your reasoning could be anything: You're exhausted from sports practice, overworked from an especially taxing week of homework, or even just totally wiped out from having to baby-sit your super-animated younger siblings. However, all of these things lead back to the fact that you just don't want to do the job. The result is . . . well, you don't; you cut enough corners to be satisfied with checking things off in your homework planner.

Here's the thing: It's okay and totally understandable that you aren't always in a work-oriented frame of mind. We know that you're probably carrying more than a full load of responsibilities, not to mention all of the extra things that come up in your life. You probably won't hear this from anyone else, but there actually are times when doing just enough is just that: enough to get you through that rough moment. However, this does not translate to our condoning the habit of just getting by. The student who does only enough work to be able to rationalize (albeit somewhat guiltily) checking off a given assignment from a to-do list is the same student who has absolutely no clue when the teacher asks him the next day in class about that checked off work.

So, what are we saying? Yes, there are times when you have to prioritize what you really need to complete thoroughly and where it might be all right to just scrape by. This depends on how you can assess your homework load. Do you have a test the following day? Are there any free periods before a given class during which you might be able to complete a less important assignment? Should you really be spending your time on the phone or gaming on your computer for two hours when you know you have to finish a paper? Avoiding something is not going to magically allow you to get by without some repercussions. There's a key point to remember if you decide to push some of your work to the bottom of the list: Do not forget to come back to it. Doing a half-hearted job of something doesn't mean you've completed it, it only means you've given yourself a freebie with an expiration date. The expiration date comes when the work you've only glossed over earlier becomes a significant portion of a graded assessment, or even your class grade overall, and it is now extremely difficult to catch up with the material. Make sure you come back to do the real work on it before this happens.

The times when you have to suck it up and bite the bullet are for those top of the list points: the test you have coming up, the essay that's due day after tomorrow, or the mid-term project report you have to turn in. Just getting it done will cost you having to accept a B when you know you could've pulled at least an A-. This just-get-by mentality extends even more deeply to those assignments that you've pushed aside in favor of the ones you've decided are worth more. If you just flip through the pages of the chapter you needed to read for English or just looked up the answers to the questions on your math assignment, you're going to have to spend more than double the time you might've invested at a first go when you're forced to relearn it for an essay or test. In middle school, your teachers try to stop you from doing this by giving pop-quizzes, but you'll find fewer of these in high school. You might be thinking, "That's definitely a good thing!" but the reality is that your high school teachers expect more from you. They believe that they shouldn't have to spoon-feed or baby-sit you in completing your work to the best of your abilities, which is true—by now, you know exactly what you need to get done and when it needs to be finished.

To prevent from falling behind, you should first be able to recognize if or when you may feel the urge to set things aside. While you should be keeping on top of your work, everyone is human and sometimes you may choose to put off doing an assignment for another day. If you know you tend to let certain assignments go, maybe even for specific classes, designate a catch up day for yourself to thoroughly address this work. If you've only skimmed over a textbook reading or filled in the blanks of a homework sheet without paying attention to what you were actually doing, go back and do it again. It might seem like extra work, but really, this is what you would've done the first time around if you'd had the time. Additionally, it will save you huge amounts of stress and time in the future when that material is included in a cumulative test.

You'll probably hear any number of old sayings about doing things in a timely fashion. Here are a few our own parents and teachers threw at us: "Just do it," "Time lost is never found again," "A stitch in time saves nine," "Never leave for tomorrow what you can do today," etc. That was all lovely to hear and a great way for them to say, "I told you so," but here's the one we've created from their input: Do what you can, while you can. And if necessary, make sure you find the time to catch up what you couldn't do!

Once you've familiarized yourself with the rhythm of your schedule and work habits, you are ready to work from the more concretely set Worksheet: Weekly Schedule. The purpose of Worksheet: Weekly Schedule is to solidify your work routine. Of course, your schedule should be flexible enough for you to actually be able to follow it. A minute-by-minute map of your day is impossible to stick to. Thus, it's important to consider your endurance throughout a work period. As the year goes on, you may find that you can

worksheet:
weekly schedule

Time	Monday	Tuesday	Wednesday	Thursday	Friday
3:30—4:15					
4:15—4:30					
4:30—4:45					
4:45 - 5:00					
5:00—5:15					
5:15—5:30					
5:30—5:45					
6:00—6:15					
6:15—6:30					
6:30—6:45					
6:45—7:00					
7:00—7:15					
7:15—7:30					
7:30—7:45					
7:45—8:00					
8:00—8:15					
8:15—8:30					
8:30—8:45					
8:45—9:00					
Time Slot:					
Saturday					
Sunday					

sit and concentrate for longer intervals without taking a break, but regardless, you'll need to take time every so often to ensure you don't burn out.

If you've gotten into the groove of keeping track of your assignments, use your planner or the provided applicable worksheets to keep track of assignments and time. This transition from a daily summary to a weekly overview is a step forward in maintaining strict Organization of your work.

To keep yourself sane and on track, it's important to consider and include the following information in your weekly schedule:

Prep time. Before beginning any homework, allow fifteen to thirty minutes to prepare materials and your workspace. Once you start working, you shouldn't have to get up to retrieve pens, calculator, dictionary, etc. All materials should be readily available for your use. The time you spend setting yourself up to work is your prep time.

Flex time. Flex time is a scheduled, fifteen-minute cushion of time that allows you maximum flexibility in your work schedule. Flex time should be included after every one or two subjects. That way, if you are spending more time than you planned on a particular assignment, need a break, or have to call a friend to clarify an assignment, you can use this scheduled break without throwing yourself off schedule. If you are completely on schedule, you can use flex time either as a brief rest or a head start on your next assignment. Flex time should also be scheduled at the end of each evening for use as extra study time for tests, work on projects or Daily Maintenance Work.

Subjects (from Worksheet: Homework Organization with Time). Transfer the subjects into the appropriate time slots based on the order of completion and duration. For example, if you complete your English homework first and spend approximately one hour on it, then write in "English" in the first four time slots of your afternoon. As your homework changes daily and you want to be able to apply the schedule in a more general manner, don't write specific homework assignments in the slots—that's what your planner is for. Make sure that you finish all the assignments for each subject without interruptions.

Dinner/Activities. Your evenings most likely consist of more than just completing your homework. Make sure to account for bigger interruptions.

Maintenance of Materials. A fifteen-minute block of time at the end of each week should be set aside for you to make sure all materials are in order and papers are filed properly.

jake

Jake comes home, exhausted from the school day. After plopping his bag next to the couch, Jake falls onto it and snags the TV remote and starts flipping channels. It's hard to believe that only a few weeks ago, he was playing soccer on the beach with his friends. Now he's stuck waking up early, sticking out the school day without getting too bored, soccer practice after school, all in addition to trying to juggle guitar lessons, chores, and homework, so his "chill time" is harder to come by. However, Jake has stuck to his resolution to keep track of his nightly homework assignments, which surprised him at how easy it makes each night's work.

Since the school year has already gotten underway, Jake has a good sense of what his schedule will be like for the rest of semester and it only looks to get busier. However, he believes that he definitely lucked out this year, since his cute neighbor and friend, Bianca, is in a bunch of his classes. Their schedules coincide in terms of academic load and extra-curricular activities, and Jake has found himself talking with Bianca more often. They've been sitting near each other in class, walking to soccer practice together, and sometimes doing homework during their shared lunch period. Even though he teases her for it, Jake is impressed by how neat and organized she is. Unfortunately, today he had a math club meeting during lunch, and missed out on his usual homework time with her.

Jake takes his bag into his room and dumps the contents onto the floor. He digs through this mass of work for his planner and sighs, looking at the seemingly massive amount of work before him to be completed. After surveying his planner, Jake realizes that he has homework assignments for all of his subjects. He pulls out his Worksheet: Homework Organization with Time and starts planning his night. He notes that it's 3:34 but jots down 3:45 in the "Start Time" slot to allow himself a few extra minutes. Jake quickly copies his assignments from his planner into the corresponding

"Assignment" column on the sheet. Once he's set himself up to work, Jake considers completing his homework in order of easiest to most difficult. He manages to talk himself out of that plan and decides to start with his least favorite subject, math, so that he can get it over and leave history or English (neither of which he minds doing) to complete at the end. He then approximates the different lengths of time that he will work on each subject. Jake has found that he usually spends anywhere between forty–five minutes to an hour and half slogging through his math homework. Thus, he fills in "1 hr 15 minutes" in the "Duration" column, figuring the averaged time is accurate enough. He estimates that each of the rest of his assignments can be completed in about forty–five minutes, with the exception of French, which he figures will only take twenty minutes.

At the end of the night, Jake yawns as he surveys his planner for any remaining tasks. Finding no remaining homework to do, he stretches and packs up his bag. Just as a feeling of achievement starts to settle in, Carolina passes by his room and halts in the door-way, startled.

"What are you doing up still? What have you been doing all night?"

"What do you mean, 'What have I been doing?' I've been working!"

"But it's way past ten. There's no way you've been working this whole time. I was just going to grab a snack before finishing up my stuff . . . dude, even I'm almost done. "

Stunned, Jake looks at the clock and realizes it is in fact almost 11 P.M. He looks at his Worksheet: Homework Organization with Time, grudgingly scribbles 10:30 in the "end time" slot, and starts to think about his evening. Although he spent as much time as planned on each assignment, he realizes that he had some, well, interrup-tions. There were several "quick" email checks, a few phone calls (that ran a bit longer than they should have), a snack break (but that barely counts because it was fruit that his mom made him eat), and dinner which extended into a TV break that lasted an hour and a half.

Irritated that he has no time left to game after he's finished his homework, Jake decides to be more mindful of his breaks starting the following day. He figures that he did properly allocate his work-time for each subject despite the evening's results, and will definitely start to plan out his work for the history project his teacher is assigning the following day. He is also determined to stick to only taking his set homework break times. Despite these resolutions, Jake is still annoyed with himself for disregarding his own careful planning. Before allowing himself to finally head to bed, he sits in his seat at his desk and flips through the guide. Glancing at the next worksheet, Jake decides to create a weekly schedule based on the Worksheet: Homework Organization with Time pages he's been filling out. He makes sure to include his afternoon soccer practices every day after school and guitar lessons on Thursdays, and incorporates these commitments into his planning accordingly. He also accepts that he must start his work later than usual on the days he has soccer matches and tournaments scheduled. His completed effort is a minute-by-minute schedule of his week, from the moment he enters the front door of his house to the time he goes to sleep. Once again feeling triumphant, he shows his work to Carolina.

Barreling into her room, Jake blurts out, "So, I made out a sheet with the weekly schedule that I'm going to follow. I'll start my homework right after a snack, work straight through until dinner, and then finish off whatever few assignments are left after I eat. What do you think?"

After being rudely startled, Carolina looks at her brother skeptically. "Um, right. What's going to happen to your schedule if you want to get a drink or if your math homework takes longer than you thought? Did you even read the directions before writing out your weekly schedule sheet?"

Jake snorts and derisively states, "All I need to do is finish one assignment after another."

"That's totally unrealistic!"

Jake falters, now unsure of his plan. "So then, what am I sup-posed to do?"

"Just read the directions. We can work from there."

"Come onnnnnn. Like you said, it's already eleven o'clock! Can't you just help me . . . please?"

Carolina sighs, "Fine. Let me see what you did." Carolina takes the sheet from Jake, quickly looking over his work. "First of all, let's start with your plan. You've got yourself working nonstop, leaving no room for yourself to even breathe! Realistically, you've got to plan in some wiggle room for yourself. First, there's the time you need when you get home and put your stuff together before doing your work. Then, you should give yourself little time gaps in between subjects. If you give yourself that timing flexibility, then you'll actually be able to follow the schedule you set up. Otherwise, you're more likely to mess up and eventually give up on it altogether."

Quietly listening to his sister's explanation, Jake now interrupts. "So, like, how much time do I give myself and when do I do that?"

Carolina sighs, and shoots her brother a tired look. "I really wish you'd just read the directions; you could've saved us both the time. You should give yourself fifteen minute time slots after every subject so that you have some 'wiggle room.'"

Jake is silent for a few seconds. "All right, I get it. So, for exam-ple, if math takes me longer than originally planned, I won't need to cut into science time that would fall immediately next?"

"Exactly. Plus, this way, if you feel like you need a break, you'll be able to take one. Or, if you've hit a good work stride, you can always start on your next assignment and might even finish earlier than planned."

Jake exhales heavily. "Yeah, okay. I get it."

"You're still forgetting something. What about Friday and the weekend?"

"Fridays I go to the movies after school, and the weekend . . . well, it's the weekend! So what?"

"Jake, it's fine to give yourself time off on Friday, but you can't act like you never have homework on the weekend! Fridays should be flex time, as in if you've got work then you do it, and if you don't have to work then you can hang out. And as far as the weekend goes, you'd better decide now when you'll do work. It's not like you do anything that important on the weekends, and you'll wind up bumming around and then freaking out at 9 P.M. on Sunday. In order to avoid a repeat performance of last weekend's mess, you should plan in time that you must spend studying."

Jake silently glowers at his now useless schedule to keep himself from resentfully glaring at his sister. Finally he sighs heavily and, sullenly glancing up at his all-knowing, expertly experienced sister Carolina, mutters, "I hate it when you're right."

"Go work and show me your schedule once you've revised it."

"Later."

"Sure, don't say thank you or anything. . . ." Carolina calls after Jake's retreating back.

Jake returns to his room, shutting the door slowly as he tiredly reviews his schedule. He decides that Friday afternoons will be a no-homework time slot because he likes to hang out with his friends after school. He figures that if he has a lot of homework or big tests coming up, he can use Friday, Saturday, and Sunday afternoons to study if necessary. As Jake is very diligent about using his planner, he doesn't use Worksheet: Academic Planner Alternative to keep track of his daily homework. Yawning, and realizing how late it is, Jake resolves to finish reworking his weekly schedule plan tomorrow and shuts off his desk lamp before climbing into bed.

Planning for Big Projects:
Papers, Quizzes, Tests, and Exams

By now, you've become a pro at managing daily assignments, or at least nearly so. The next step is effectively applying the Time Management techniques you've acquired to bigger projects and tests. These bigger projects can range in size and vary in form for each subject, from weekly analytical overview papers to chapter or unit tests, and even to final exams. The most important lesson in managing larger assignments is learning to break up your work into manageable portions. When given any assignment, you should review the expectations, divide the work into smaller sections, and use your academic planner, Worksheet: Academic Planner Alternative, or calendar to allow time to do each task segment. We will go through this process for all manner of bigger projects.

Writing Assignments:
Book Reports, Essays, and Papers

This type of big project ranges from a third grade book report to an eleventh grade term paper, and these particular assignments require more time and energy investment to complete than any other. You will need to consider all aspects of the assigned project, from the Pre-project work to the actual writing and production of the final draft, and decide how much time you dedicate to each step of this process. Each writing project can be divided or broken down into five parts:

1. Pre-project setup. The most important aspect that sets the tone for your project is a thorough and full understanding of what you have been assigned. The Pre-project stage is a two-tiered stage in which you will set the pace for your assignment: Brainstorming and Time Planning. Brainstorming is anything that you do before you actually set out to work on your project. This step involves knowing and comprehending what the assignment requires of you, picking a topic, and figuring out a general direction for your project based on the type of Research or analysis involved. This step allows you to later select the relevant, specific information you need for your paper from all of the Research you acquire.

The Time Planning step is exactly what it sounds like—planning out how exactly you will spend your time, from the date you first receive the assignment to its final due date. This project is most likely not your only school work, so it's important to carefully consider how to designate your time. You should take into consideration any additional required sub-deadlines (like an Outline, first or subsequent drafts, or bibliography due dates) and the final due date of your project.

Decide how long you will need to spend on each of the following steps: Research, drafting, and Editing. Keep in mind the sub-deadlines (if necessary) and the amount of other subjects' coursework also assigned, and set due dates for yourself. Here, of course, you must act as your own boss in keeping your word regarding the deadlines you set for yourself. The best way to keep on top of your work is to include the particular work you've set for yourself in your daily homework assignment planner. Once you've created a project schedule, integrate your due dates into your general calendar or academic planner. We have provided Worksheet: Monthly Calendar for planning bigger projects and exam studying, but a purchased desk or wall calendar or the calendar in your academic planner can be used in the same way. The idea is to be able to glance at the worksheet or calendar as planned and remember bigger chunks of work that need to be completed.

2. Research is the backbone of your project. This step is the key component to backing up anything and everything you say in your paper, so be sure to get your hands on as many facts as possible! You can always pare down the amount of information you gather when you begin the writing process. You may need to thoroughly read a novel, visit a local or school library to find a particular document, or interview someone to serve as primary source. Regardless of topic or course subject, the Research component of your project is just as important as the actual writing. Make sure to designate sufficient time in your Time Planning to be able to fully Research your subject before you even sit down to write. If you are having trouble figuring out how to Research, make sure to ask someone for help. Your teacher, school or local librarian, or a parent can help.

Now that you have all of this information, you are probably itching to write it all down. Don't rush to the computer and type up everything you've learned. Instead, take the time to go through your Brainstorm and Research notes, and decide what information you want to include and the order in which to present it- these components will be written up in your Outline. Make sure that you have an organized and cohesive plan for how to write your paper. Be as detailed as you'd like in your Outline, even including writing down which facts should appear where. The more you put into this step, the easier the actual writing process will be. Once you've completed your Outline, you can begin the actual writing process.

3. First Draft. Make sure to keep your Outline close by at all times when putting together your First Draft. Remember all the effort and intentions that you devoted to creating the Outline and use it to guide your writing. After you've completed your First Draft, put it away for a day or two. Nobody writes a perfect First Draft. In fact, the fewer drafts you have, the more work you may have to invest in each draft to perfect your piece. Come back to your initial draft and read over everything that you've written.

4. Edit and make any appropriate changes. You can even swap assignments with a friend when possible and work as one another's Editors. It's amazing what a different pair of eyes may find or what a fresh point of view can contribute to the quality of your work.

worksheet:
paper planning

Part of Project	Duration	My Due Date	Class Due Date
Pre-project			
Notes:			
Research			
Notes:			
Outlining			
Notes:			
Draft 1			
Notes:			
Draft 2			
Notes:			
Final Edit			
Notes:			

jake and bianca

Bianca writes down the evening's math assignments in her planner while the teacher wraps up the day's class, also noting that she'd previously marked today as a start date for an upcoming English project. She scans her planner's monthly calendar and is reminded of her upcoming soccer tournament. Feeling a moment of panic, she frantically considers when she can fit in all of her schoolwork assignments. School has always been the top priority for Bianca, and she has worked hard to maintain good grades. Since she was a little girl, Bianca has dreamed of following in her mom's footsteps to attend Wellesley College. Bianca is especially pleased to have been elected class secretary of her eighth grade class, and takes great pride in her ability to balance her schoolwork, soccer, and various extracurricular and social commitments. However, figuring out exactly how to balance these things tends to make her totally anxious.

At the ring of the bell, Bianca gathers her books and glances at Jake, who appears to still be conked out (as he has been since five minutes into class). She rolls her eyes, and grinning wickedly to herself, heads out of class to the English department office. She wants to make absolutely sure that she understands the English assignment that accounts for a third of this trimester's grade. Bianca meets briefly with her teacher, and satisfied with her solid understanding of the English project, heads back out to study a little during her free period. As she walks toward the library, she nearly trips when she is startled by Jake, who has managed to shake off his coma and is now rushing down the hall while yelling her name, brushing aside his buddies in order to catch up with her. Jake continues to shout after her, "Yo, B! Bianca! Hey wait up!"

Jake, still winded from his sprint and ignoring the comments from his friends, manages to cough out, "Hey, wanna come over to my house today after practice?" At seeing her startled expression from having been caught off guard, he hastily explains, "Oh, I really want, I mean I was wondering if we could work together on the math homework."

Bianca considers for a moment then suggests, "Why don't we meet at the library instead. I want to start to work on the English project, and since last time we tried working at my house, and we ended up gaming more than actually working, it's probably better if we studied at the library." Jake hurriedly agrees, turning to let Bianca walk in front of him, and trails after her before he realizes his friends are watching him expectantly. Remembering that he had promised to play a short pick-up game with the guys during their free period, Jake forces himself to stop mid-step. "All right," he calls after Bianca. "Sweet, I'll text you when I'm on my way."

Jake meets Bianca at the library several hours later around 5:30 P.M., after having wrapped up soccer practice and gone home to clean up a bit. Upon entering, Jake is still distracted and driven by the adrenaline of his soccer practice and game prospects, while Bianca has already turned her attention to their homework assignment. After wandering aisles for a few moments, they find a large and secluded table to work at, each choosing a side to spread out their work. Bianca removes her agenda book from her school bag to number the order in which she will complete her homework. Jake, seeing that Bianca is already in business mode, shows her the schedule that he created with Carolina the night before. Bianca is astonished and somewhat impressed, and the two decide to use Jake's very useful schedule to base their day's work on, starting together with the math assignment. They each complete all of their assignments, taking small five-minute breaks between each subject.

After they check off all the day's assigned homework, Jake begins to gather his books and pack up. Bianca looks at him in surprise and exclaims, "Hey, we're not done yet."

Jake freezes in the middle of shoving his planner into his bag. "What do you mean we aren't done?"

"Well, we still have to look at the English project."

"No we don't. That's not due for another four weeks."

"Don't you think we should look at the assignment and check-out those suggested readings Mr. Z mentioned in class and take notes?" Bianca prompts, pushing her own notebook forward to indicate the aforementioned pages.

"What for? I have notes from class and I already know what I'm going to write about," Jake frowns, resuming his packing. "Plus, the Outline's not due for another two weeks."

Bianca shrugs and returns her attention to her books. "Oooooh-kay, whatever. I'm gonna stay to do some more work because this is a huge paper."

Jake straightens and retorts, "I'm not going to cram! But there's no point in doing this work now when we've got plenty of time!" The two cringe and apologize when a passing librarian shushes them.

Bianca shakes her head. "Whatever you say," she whispers, turning back to resume her work. "I don't know about you, but with final championships, regionals, and states, I'm not willing to risk it."

Jake fidgets with his bag straps, hesitating. "Want me to walk you home?" he offers hopefully.

"No, that's okay. I'll get my mom to pick me up. Thanks though," Bianca chirps without breaking her concentration from studying her planner.

Jake shifts nervously, and turns grudgingly to leave. "All right. See you tomorrow."

Jake waves at Bianca as he slouches down the aisle toward the exit. Bianca grins momentarily to herself as she sees Jake's back-pack disappear from view around the stacks, and returns her focus to her notebook and calendar to make a game plan for the English paper. Although Jake is right about not having to hand anything in for at least two weeks, she wants to understand the components of the paper and figure out when to start the rough draft. She flips to a blank page and concentrates on the Pre-project setup. She decides that if she can Brainstorm on the topic of her paper within the next three days, and then map out the days when she can work on the Research and writing, then she'll definitely have enough time to hand in her First Draft for a preliminary review and conference with Mr. Z. Carefully, Bianca fills out Worksheet: Paper Planning and inserts the page into her planner, which she decides to preempt and jump start her Brainstorming as soon as she gets home. As she packs up her bag, she sees Carolina checking out some books and makes her way over to say hello.

Carolina turns when Bianca touches her arm, saying pleasantly, "Hey, Bianca. Wow, you look tired."

Bianca grins, dropping her bag heavily. "I am. Coach gave us a rough time at soccer practice, and then I had to get through all my homework and some other stuff."

Carolina smiles knowingly. "Huh. I think Jake's been home playing videogames for the past hour. That boy could definitely learn a thing or two from you."

Bianca smiles back. "Well, I just wanted to figure out when I'm going to work on this English paper. It's not due for a while, but I'm a little worried because it's a huge part of our grade."

Carolina's eyebrows shoot up, and she leans back on the check-out counter. "You know, I think you're stressing yourself out too much. Look, if you did all your other work and you're on top of the material, you'll be fine. You seem like you've already got a workable plan in mind, so stick to it and pace yourself. There's no need to kill yourself when you've got enough on your plate as it is! "

Somewhat relieved at hearing this from the junior class valedictorian, Bianca asks, "Are you sure?"

Carolina grabs her library books, and responds, "Yes, I'm sure. You'll be fine. Stick to your study schedule, and I'm sure you'll be fine!"

"Thanks, Carolina. Hey, maybe I'll actually get in a game or two of my own tonight."

Carolina laughs and heads for the door, "You could definitely use the break, Bianca! See you later."

Planning to Study for Quizzes and Tests

Along with daily and long-term assignments, you will also have to plan to study for quizzes and tests. Flipping through your notes the day before the exam does not constitute studying, and thinking about studying certainly doesn't count either. Let's take a look at how to break down your study plan.

Get the Facts. As soon as your teacher even hints at the possibility of an upcoming test, make a note in your planner. Write down all the information you are given about the test, including test date, format, length, and concepts to be tested.

Get Organized. Once you have the exam information, you are ready to begin the planning process. We will address how to study in Chapter 6, so for now let's focus on how to formulate your study schedule. Organize your notes and consider the information your teacher provided.

Get Real About Timing. Based on the amount of information you will be tested on and your familiarity with the subject content, you should plan to dedicate two to five study days for preparation. If you are getting ready for a test in a subject that you do well in, you will probably need less study time than for a subject that requires more work from you. When you've determined the duration of your prep, take a look at your Worksheet: Monthly Calendar (see pages 96–97) or your wall calendar, consider what other work you have scheduled for each day, and then add in the daily study goals leading up to the exam.

Keep the Test in Mind. Make sure that you include times to meet with your teachers to address trouble spots or to meet with your friends for study dates.

jake and carolina

Jake was informed last week of two tests set for this Thursday (math and science), and his English teacher spontaneously decided to give a vocabulary quiz on Friday. Keeping all this in mind, Jake starts to create a study schedule, referring to his desk calendar, and marking off the test dates. Jake decides he'll study on Wednesday night for the two tests on Thursday, as he resigns himself to a long night of work, then decides to give himself an early break for a few rounds of gaming.

Seemingly on cue, Carolina walks into Jake's room. "What's that?" she asks.

"It's my test schedule. I made it so that I can study for my tests on time. And I've already done most of my homework for tonight."

Carolina leans forward to inspect the sheet. "How exactly did you determine how much time to spend studying for each test?" Closer inspection of Jake's schedule causes Carolina to suddenly straighten in disbelief. "Wait, are you seriously just going to study the night before each test??"

Jake looks at his sheet and sputters, "Well, yeah. I mean, I've got all my stuff, and all I need to do is read through it before each test."

Carolina stares at her brother. "Jake, we've been through this. That is not studying. You need to actually make time enough in advance to go through all your materials before you even sit down to study it!"

"Yeah, so? I only need the day before the test for that! What's the big deal anyway?"

"Let's start with the fact that you randomly chose study time length for each subject. Did you even look to see if you've got review sheets for each test? How about going through your notes to decide how much time you'll need to thoroughly go through the material for those classes? What happens if soccer runs over or your coach decides to have a double practice last minute and you're stuck with no time to study?"

Jake waves his hands at his sister, hoping to shoo away the truth, muttering, "Yeah, yeah, okay!"

"Jake, you're not even listening."

"Because you're being ridiculous. I don't need to do all that."

"Look, you're good at history, but not so good that you don't need to plan out your studying more carefully. It is totally unrealistic to assume that you're able to study for two tests the night before them, let alone one, and then somehow cram in some vocab review after soccer practice for another quiz the next day. You're overextending yourself. Are you planning on not sleeping from Wednesday to Friday? Because that's what it looks like according to this."

Jake slouches in his desk chair, taking in the scenario that Carolina has bluntly, but accurately, described. "So then what am I supposed to do?"

"I already told you. Luckily, today is Monday. You should spend today gathering all review sheets, notes, and any worksheets for each of the tests. This also helps you figure out if you don't have a specific sheet or set of notes. For those subjects, look through all of your materials and decide which specific areas are more difficult. You're gonna need more time to review these topics than those that you're more comfortable with. Estimate how much time you'll need to study in total based on tonight's assessment, and then think about how many days before each test you should start studying. As for the vocab quiz, you can start studying for that today. Just pick five or so words to learn each night, depending on how many in total you need to know for the quiz, and each day, starting today, keep reviewing them up until the quiz. You should have gotten through all of the words two nights before the quiz so that the night before, all you need to do is some simple review."

Jake gnaws on his inner cheek, taking in Carolina's advice, then blurts, "Well, I don't even get anything that we're doing in science, so what am I supposed to do about that?"

"Just do what I said before—go through all your material tonight and pick out the topics that you are most confused about, and then write out any questions you have about those things. Definitely go talk to your teacher tomorrow, before or after class. If you have a whole bunch of questions, or your teacher sees that you're really confused, then set up a time to meet for longer so that you can really work through it. The rest of the prep is on you, and we've already gone over what you need to do."

"But I have questions about everything. I told you, I don't get what we're learning!"

"Jake, that's a total cop-out and you know it. Did you bother reading your textbook yet, let alone review any of your class notes?"

Jake is silent, desperately wishing that Carolina could have offered an easier plan, "Not yet. So . . . fine, I get it. More work. Fun. Awesome."

Carolina pats Jake's shoulder, angling her head to catch his eye. "Come on, you have plenty of time to figure out what you need to focus on more, and still get through all of the material. Like I said—it's Monday, so just get started now. The sooner you start, the easier you can get through it all." With this Carolina strolls out of Jake's room, and leaves him to start pulling textbooks and binders from his bag and pluck a fresh sheet of paper to revise his study schedule.

worksheet:
monthly calendar

Create your own calendar if you do not want to use an existing monthly calendar.

MONTH:

Sunday	Monday	Tuesday	Wednesday	Thursday	Friday	Saturday

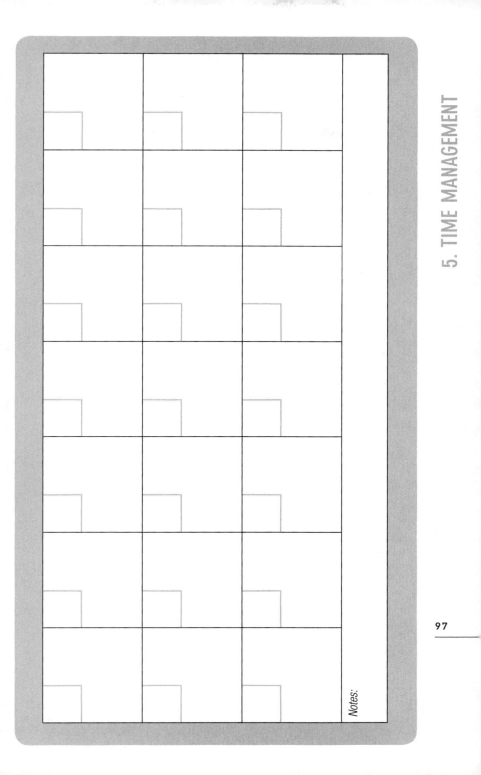

Notes:

Planning Midterm and Finals Prep

The steps we present here are similar to those discussed in the section on test preparation, as seen with Worksheet: Monthly Calendar. However studying for midterms and finals requires extra time and more thorough prep work. Studying for cumulative exams will require advanced planning. Usually, studying for a midterm or final type exam should begin three to four weeks before the test date.

"Break It Up" Midterm and Finals Prep

1. **Get the Facts.** As with regular test prep you should begin by gathering the necessary information and materials including, notes, old tests, handouts and review sheets.

2. **Get Organized.** Make a list of all the topics that will be covered on the test. Use Worksheet: What I Know (see facing page) and consider the range of the topics, how well you understand and remember, and how quickly you will be able to review the information.

3. **Get Real About Timing.** Use your Worksheet: Monthly Calendar, agenda planner, or desk calendar to record information about the following steps. Decide how much time will need to be dedicated to each topic based on Worksheet: What I Know. Divide into four weeks of review

   Weeks 1 and 2—daily review of topics (see Chapter 9, "The Study Devices to Make It All Stick")

   Week 3—create practice tests and meet with teachers

   Week 4—final review and practice tests

worksheet:
what i know

Strong Spots	Iffy Spots	Trouble Spots

CHAPTER 6

Study Skills:
Literally, How to Learn Stuff

Studying" is another one of those words with the dangerous potential for being misinterpreted as an empty, meaningless term. For example, many a student can recall a situation where a parent yells, "Why don't you go to your room and study instead of [fill in the blank]?!" To avoid such situations, we might as well address the problem of what exactly they mean. When we discuss "studying," we aren't just referring to those couple of nights before a test that you spend reviewing notes and cramming information into your head.

Studying is the method by which you learn stuff. This includes all work you invest in a subject: both class and book notes you take, homework you complete, the Daily Maintenance Work you perform to manage this material, and those nights you spend poring over all of the above to create study guides for tests. How well you are able to study manifests in how effectively you can apply all of what you've learned, not just in a test setting, but under any circumstances. If you've studied well, we should be able to wake you up at 3 A.M. to ask you, for example, to describe the processes of cellular respiration and photosynthesis and have you respond, sleepily but accurately and in great detail.

Here again, many students will shrug, thinking something to the effect of, "So what, who cares about learning school stuff? It's not like any of it is useful in real life. . . ." Let us save you the time of this argument: This is not true. Regardless of your chosen future path, no individual can succeed in any field without basic knowledge of the world. No matter what you chose to do professionally, you still need to know such things as basic mathematic calculations or simple facts about world or U.S. history. Having such knowledge in your personal arsenal can give you that satisfied feeling of being able to understand such things as the joke, "Your epidermis is showing," while others may not.

Studying also has the added (and more subtle) benefit of training your brain how to learn. This may sound weird, but in order to have the best butterfly kick in the soccer arena or be the unbeatable lawyer in a courtroom, you need to know which techniques work best for you to practice the skills you need. Learning how you learn best will be your biggest asset no matter what you do.

You may find throughout the year that the time you spend studying follows a pattern that can be depicted much like a titration curve, for you chemists. At the beginning of the school term, you may need only a minimal amount of study time to prepare sufficiently to do well on tests, because the material covered is mainly a review of things you've already learned. However, as the year progresses, you'll find yourself devoting more and more time to studying, as new concepts are introduced and reinforced by maintenance preparation for tests. Finally, as you near the end of the term, you might notice that your study times have leveled off to an average, as you've practiced and honed your Study Skills to the point where they are essentially habits. Of course, each person learns differently, so everyone's learning curve is unique.

Obviously, you will need the means to get to this point. Before you even begin prepping for a test, there are important steps that you should be taking. As you read through our suggestions, you may feel like we're proposing a lot of extra work, but in reality these study techniques will enhance your current approach and allow you a much less painful test prep process. The extra plus of working through these steps is that you'll feel more prepared and confident during your classes.

Class Notes

Your classes are the first source of new material that you encounter. Thus, the notes you take during class are a recording of your first exposure to this material. Your goal in taking class notes is to gather as many accurate details as you can from what your teacher says. Despite what your personal opinions may be and regardless of which class you consider, your teachers really do want you to succeed and they do not make their tests harder than the level at which they present the material. Actually, you'll probably find that during class, your teachers emphasize what you will need to focus on for either the homework assigned for the particular session or the upcoming test of the material covered. By taking class notes, you'll also force yourself to be attentive to the things going on in the course of a period. You will engage your mind by actively writing down notes on what's being said and be less likely to allow your mind to wander.

What to Write Down . . . and Yes, It's Important to *Write* it Down

The things you should jot down are actually fairly easy to recognize. Anything your teacher has pre-written on the board or on an overhead should be copied exactly and as soon as it's presented. This means, if there's stuff up as soon as you enter the classroom, make sure you immediately write it down as soon as you're situated. It's important to actually be listening to what is being said in class; this includes anything your teacher highlights as being important, even comments that your fellow classmates may make.

The bulk of taking good class notes lies in being able to hear what's being said, and thus, pick out the "jewels" of key points made. Translation: Eighty percent of your attention should be invested in listening, and the remaining twenty percent devoted to scribbling the significant ideas down.

Teachers lecture in somewhat different ways but ultimately have the same fundamental aim. If your teacher tends to present concepts in the form of questions, you should take note of what he or she is asking and what is recognized as the correct answer, as there is likely a very specific reason the teacher wants to point out this information. Similarly, if your teacher indicates that a particular homework question or reading passage is "a good one," this should translate in your mind to "potential test question or material." This is especially true for any passages, questions, or concepts you've marked as troublesome to answer or significant. In a more discussion-based class, like English, foreign language literature or history classes, any discussion that takes up at least a large portion of an entire class, or which even more than one class period is dedicated to investigating, should be noted with special attention to those points that your teacher underscores.

Keep in Mind:

» Date each page

» Write down any information that your teacher repeats

» Copy over facts that are written on the board

» Listen eighty percent of the time and take notes twenty percent of the time

Class Notes for Those Who Hate Taking Notes

If you absolutely hate the idea of taking notes during class, or feel like you cannot listen and write copious notes, you should realize that this doesn't mean that you should not have anything written down from class. Remember that what is covered in class is useful for the learning process and you do want to walk away remembering the information. So if you feel that you remember more by listening, or think that you miss too much trying to juggle writing and listening, then consider bringing a recorder to the class. Get permission from the teacher and take your recorder to class and set it up somewhere that will have a clear pick up of the lecture. In the meantime, you can listen during the class and take just a few notes. These notes could be limited to a page of important information that your teacher wrote on the board or things you want to review after class. As with written notes, you should write the date and the topic so that you can go back and reference the discussion.

Your work is not done after you've recorded your notes, however. The trick to taking recorded notes is that you must listen to the notes over and over again. Strap on your headphones and repeatedly listen to each class lecture. This method doesn't really work that well for math or science, so save it for history, foreign language (or literature), and English! What works best for math or science is practicing and reworking example problems or homework questions, and talking your way through them as you go along.

Reading vs. Reading to Learn

For many years, your parents and teachers insisted that you read for fun. With much enthusiasm, books with pretty covers and interesting titles were put into your hands. Perhaps you caught the reading bug and find yourself staying up late leafing through pages of a new find, or maybe you're doing the compulsory thirty-minute stints to appease your mother. In either case, you're reading for the story, the action, the practice . . . and you should keep reading! However, for school you will need to do a different type of reading—reading to learn stuff. The process of active reading to derive important information, interpret characters, or uncover underlying themes is an integral part of the learning process. You'll be moving away from just reading and toward reading with the intention to learn from what you're reading. We'll explore the activity of reading technical books such as history and science textbooks and engaging in books that you encounter in your literature and English classes. Remember that while you can still just sit back and enjoy a good read (in and out of school) the reading that you will do for your classes is a more involved process from which you will gather information and teach yourself about new topics.

Reading Textbooks

Reading is a crucial component to the study process. Many students disregard any text reading or reading packet assignments as optional, figuring that the material will be covered in class anyway, so why bother? Since you're not one of these students, you know that, while yes, material may be introduced in class, the bulk of class time is spent going into depth about the material instead of covering the basics. Therefore, in order to be able to understand what is going on, the reading is essential.

Notes You Take on Textbooks

Reading is a huge chunk of your homework assignments. If your teacher has assigned you to read a chapter and answer questions at the end of the reading, then he probably expects that you will actually read the text. Therefore, if you're simply looking at the question and then finding the answer in the reading, you aren't really doing your homework. Actually doing your homework, especially for your history, science and English reading assignments, is about active reading and taking book notes while reading. Active reading involves more than just looking at words. You may find it helpful to preview any end of chapter questions before you dive into the reading, as this may help target your review of the assigned pages.

Before you even start looking at the words (let alone putting pen to paper) you should survey each page. Start by reading over the headings of the chapter. Look at how the chapter is broken up, which words are in bold, and which topics are given special attention with charts and pictures. Ask yourself what you think the reading will be about. While it might seem like an extra step, it is helpful to take a few seconds to orient yourself, like clearing the path before you start walking. Once you have a sense of the reading, you can begin actually reading. Break up the material into small segments; this may be as short as a paragraph or two. Read each segment at your normal reading pace. Don't try to pick out important facts or hone in on details. For now you want to get an overview. You may consider reading the passage out loud to hear the words. Having read the section once, you should summarize what you read about. Again, you can simply review the reading in your head and summarize in one or two sentences what the section was about. Now that you have an idea of the passage, you can begin taking notes.

Re-read the same section and note important information. This does not mean that you should copy every sentence from the book, because that would just waste your time; someone's already written the book for you, after all. Book notes are a condensed translation in your own words of what you've read—a summary and some main points that popped out at you, such as important dates, people, and themes. These notes can be in bullet-point or Outline format, on a separate sheet of paper, or even in your textbook, whichever method you prefer and will be easily referenced for future studying. Our favorite note-taking method is the Outline format that allows you to look at bigger picture by asking a question and then noting details with supporting evidence.

Here's how you can use the textbook to take notes:

I. Read the main heading.
   A. Designate line with consecutive Roman numeral.
   B. Write title of heading next to Roman numeral.
      i. Turn the heading of the text into a question.
      ii. For example, if the heading is "The First Americans," the question could be "Who were the First Americans?"
   C. Indent and label the line with consecutive capital letter.
      i. Designate letter with information pertaining to evidence such as:
         1. Important idea/name/date/key word.
         2. Anything that is bold.
         3. Add information from primary source and class notes.
      ii. Limit information to topics found under the heading.
   D. Indent and label line with Arabic (normal) number any details/examples from information in capital letter.
   E. Repeat steps A—E for each paragraph.
   F. Make sure that the points answer the question in the Roman numeral.
II. Keep in Mind
   A. Importance of information decreases as indent increases.
      i. Major points are placed farthest to left.
      ii. More specific information is written to the right.
   B. Do not leave a hanging indentation—if you have an A then you must have a B, if you have a 1 then you must have a 2, etc.

It may take you some time to become an outline pro, but once you've got the hang of it, outlining is an excellent way of to keep yourself organized and create a systematic note taking process. To give you a sense of what your outline should look like refer to our Table of Contents which we wrote in Outline form or the sample notes, below, that we took from a segment of our history textbook on World War I.

I. What were the causes of World War I?
    A. Breakdown of several European alliances that were created by Otto von Bismarck
        i. 1879 Dual Alliance of German Empire and Austria-Hungary
        ii. 1882 Triple Alliance of German Empire, Austria-Hungary, and Italy
        iii. Peace between German Empire and the rest of Europe
    B. Kaiser Wilhelm II comes to power
        i. Doesn't support the Alliances
        ii. Creates strain in Europe
    C. Rift increases between Europe
        i. Russia, France, and British Empire come together
        ii. 1907 Triple Entente is formed
        iii. Counteract force of Triple Alliance
    D. Austria-Hungary annexes Bosnia-Herzegovina
        i. Russia is very unhappy
            1. Bosnia-Herzegovina has a large Slavic population
            2. Feels that its power is being challenged
            3. Starts destabilizing power
        ii. Region is very tense and new/different borders are created
            1. Albania
            2. Serbia
            3. Romania
            4. Bulgaria

E. Turning point is a Bosnian-Serb student kills Archduke Franz Ferdinand of Austria
  i. Austria thinks that Serbian government is involved
    1. Declares ultimatum of war
    2. Serbia cannot meet requirement
  ii. Russia jumps in and declares war on Austria-Hungary
    1. Defends Serbia
    2. Maintains power in the region
  iii. Germany becomes involved
    1. Declares war on Russia
    2. Defends Austria-Hungary

II. What were the major battles of World War I?

These notes, in addition to your notes and handouts from class, become especially handy when making study sheets for future tests and exams.

Highlighting/underlining is another way to make sure certain ideas or facts pop out at you, but beware of becoming highlighter happy—you'll know if you've gone down this path when the entire page has turned fluorescent yellow, pink, blue, or whatever color marker you hold in your hand.

natalia and bianca

Natalia had breezed through her elementary school years without giving much thought to the learning process. School, as far as she was concerned, was a place to see her friends, make it through classes without getting into trouble with her teachers for talking, socialize with fellow members from the drama club, and simply pass the time until theater class and drama club meetings. Nat never particularly minds going to school, but she much prefers to be at the Springfield Playhouse and on stage, where she can spend hours perfecting her performances. Her only goal has been to make it to her break into a Broadway show or as a star in Hollywood.

Nat goes to school mainly so that she can voice her opinions and showcase her acting skills. She is usually the first one picked for projects that involve acting or singing and is more than happy to read out loud in class. Because the teachers in her small elementary school repeatedly described Nat as "pleasure to have in class," she feels that a few solid comments and energetic participation in class are enough to get by. Nat doesn't much care about what grades she receives, and places much more weight on the remarks of her voice teacher and acting coach.

While she never thinks of memorizing lines for her plays as work, the story of her experience with Social Studies is completely different. In this particular topic, she feels only minute enthusiasm for the novels assigned. And the idea of memorizing random trivial facts, such as names and dates of important historical figures and events, is, in Nat's opinion, a waste of her time. She really doesn't care to remember who the thirty-third president was, nor does she want to learn about the events that led up to the signing of the Declaration of Independence. Nat has carried this lackadaisical attitude toward her studies into the current school year, and it seems to her that all the hype regarding the transition from one grade to another is, well, nothing more than hype. That is, until she receives her first graded papers in her Social Studies class.

Nat has functioned in this year's Social Studies class in the same manner as in her previous years' Social Studies courses. She tries to pay attention in class, but the monotone voice of her teacher sometimes makes her fall asleep, and she only completes her homework questions when she can remember what homework has been assigned. As always, she isn't totally lost, but often finds herself wondering how her classmates know the answers to the convoluted questions that her teacher poses in class. Nevertheless, Nat figures she is getting by, despite the mediocre grades she receives, until her return home late one afternoon, when her mom presents her with a mailed progress report warning, saying she is in danger of failing.

Having just left a successful play practice, Nat is totally unprepared for her mother's pointed, questions regarding exactly how she prepares for Social Studies class. As she faces question after question about highlighting, notes, and reading, Nat can only mutter that she does her homework every night by reading the questions and finding the answers within the assigned reading. Nat's mom says, "Nat, I think it's time you changed the way you go about your studying."

After this conversation with her mom, Nat takes the ugly progress report and her backpack, containing her most recently returned paper, to her room and dejectedly flicks on her computer. As she sits down to review her Social Studies paper, a chat message pops up on her screen:

```
Jshapp88: heyy! whats up.
```

Glancing at her paper and starting to type a response, Nat figures she can look over her paper while talking to her friend from the Playhouse.

```
ddramaqueen: nm. hbu?

Jshapp88: nothing really . . . r u trying out for
beast????
```

```
ddramaqueen: i shud hope so!!! i cant wait for
saturday the photog will be there taking da pic of
us for grease

jshapp88: sweeeeet! wheres that gonna be

ddramaqueen: i don't even know XD

ddramaqueen: they told us but with my memory i
have no clu

jshapp88: LOLOL you gotta write it down jk

ddramaqueen: haha. haha. truee(:
```

Just as Nat hits enter, another message popped up on her screen, this one from her ever-super-responsible sister, Bianca:

```
BibiC02: dude, what are you doing online?

ddramaqueen: im reading my social studies paper

BibiC02: I'm coming over to look at it with you
```

Before Nat can even come up with a reply, Bianca appears in her doorway with a pen and a clean notebook. Bianca sits down next to Nat at her desk as her little sister quickly swipes at the computer monitor to turn it off, and starts to examine the Nat's paper and class materials. After a seemingly endless review of every page of her class notes, homework sheets, and graded assignments, Bianca finally looks up and nods reassuringly at her.

Only furthering Nat's bafflement at her sister's reaction to such an awful mark, Bianca suggests, "Maybe I can give you a couple of hints on how you can up your grades in Social Studies. However," she says, "I am only interested in helping you when you're ready to change your attitude."

While Nat feels that there's nothing really wrong with her attitude, she finally admits to Bianca she's not sure how to fix her problems, or what they really are to begin with. She reminds Bianca that as far as she is concerned, "There is really no point to learning this stuff, and it makes no sense how the teacher even picks the topics that we end up discussing in class!"

After a brief glance at a shelf where Nat keeps her books, Bianca said, "Why don't we start by talking about your book notes? Or rather, your lack of notes. . . ."

"Because I don't need to take book notes! I already know what the chapter is about because I read it, and I can answer all of the homework questions."

Ignoring her, Bianca continues. "Every night you should skim over the assigned chapter. This means briefly reading over everything, including the headings and looking at the pictures. When you're done, you can fill me in on the overview, and we can read the chapter and take more specific notes on the reading together."

"But what's the point? The teacher never even talks about the stuff in the textbook," Nat breaks in, even more irritated at having to do so much extra work.

Bianca frowns slightly, causing Nat to abruptly shut her mouth. "Your book notes won't be a word-for-word copy of the textbook. Some very smart people were nice enough to write it all out for you already. What we're going to do is take the time necessary to fully understand what the reading says, and write down the important information."

Unable to stop herself, Nat blurts out dramatically, "Look, I don't have time to read the chapter more than once! I mean, I do have homework in other subjects that I actually care about, why bother doing so much extra work on this stuff? Plus, how am I supposed to know what's 'important'?"

"Nat, by taking notes on your textbook reading, you'll have a better idea of the discussion topics so that when you're in class, you'll actually be able to participate better in discussions. You'll probably realize that your teacher is focusing on specific parts of the previous night's reading and you'll know to take notes on those points in class. Whatever, we'll talk more about your class notes later. When you come home, you'll be able to make better sense of your reading because you kept up in class."

"All right, I get it, I get it . . . ," Nat interjects.

Sighing heavily and clearly losing patience with her sister, Bianca continues slowly, "You'll also be able to use the book notes to study from when it comes time to writing papers and preparing for quizzes."

"Yeah, that sounds awesome . . . except that this is a lot of extra work."

Bianca pauses and says flatly, "Nat, this isn't 'extra' work. You know how you're usually scrambling to figure out what to study for your tests and quizzes, and spending lots of time figuring out where to find the right information when you're getting ready to write a paper? Don't give me that face, it's on the report card. Yes, Mom showed me. Stop pretending like you couldn't tell. Not to mention the fact that I've seen you do these things myself. Anyway, my point is that all of the book notes you take will eventually be study aids."

Nat glares down at her textbook. "How does that work?"

"Here, let me show you. Open up your book to the reading for this weekend. Hang on, let me grab my pen and some paper." Rolling her eyes, Nat reaches for her textbook and flips to the pages that were assigned to review for the upcoming week.

Bianca explains, "The first thing you'll need to do is skim over the pages to figure out what you're going to be reading about. Look for anything in bold, check out the pictures and captions, and read any sidebars."

"Mmhmm . . ." Nat mutters, her thoughts drifting elsewhere.

"I don't just mean that this is something you'll do in the future. I mean right now. Skim over the pages. I'm going to see when dinner is, and when I get back, we'll move to the next step," Bianca replies as she gets up and leaves Nat alone with her Social Studies text.

Several minutes later, she returns to find Nat with her feet up on the chair she had occupied, once again rapidly typing messages to her friends. "Right. So, I hope you've gotten a basic idea of what you'll encounter in the chapter. The next step is to carefully read each section. After you read each section, you'll turn the headings into questions, and then underneath, write out the important information that answers the question you made."

Jolted back to a more alert state, Nat asks, "How do I know which information is important though?"

"Well, first try rewording the heading in the textbook into question form. From there, you need to answer that question with in-depth info that you find within the section. In other words, if you were asked the question, like for an essay or a test, then you would need to be able to write down all of the relevant information necessary to give a full answer—that's the stuff you'll be making notes on."

Nat, seeing the logic to this approach, slowly drawls, "Oookay, I think I get it."

Bianca teases, "Oookay then, let's give it a try. Where's the first heading?"

Nat leisurely drags a piece of paper over as Bianca resumes her seat beside Nat. Nat looks over the current page of the textbook. She glances at the heading and turns it into a question. Suddenly, her eyes light up as she recognizes that this was the exact discussion question listed on the syllabus for Monday's class.

Grinning up at her, she stutters at her sister and gestures at the syllabus, "Um. So, I look . . . ?"

Bianca smiles back at Nat, saying, "Hey, you might still not love Social Studies by the time we're done working together, but at least you'll actually know some of it."

Reading Literature

If you're enjoying the book that you're reading, or are not finding it particularly challenging, then just keep reading. You may consider taking notes in the margins, putting your ideas on a sticky-note, or jotting down some thoughts in your notebook. However, if you're getting through the chapters and making sense of the reading, keep going, but try to slow down so that you are reading at a pace that isn't as fast as when you're say flipping through a magazine. Make sure that you don't gloss over anything and read carefully. Once you're done with a section or chapter, write some notes about the characters, themes, and any questions that you may want to ask in class. Even if you think you'll remember the reading perfectly, taking down some notes will be helpful in the future.

If you aren't lucky enough to breeze through your reading, don't give up. Everyone, at one moment or another has re-read the same few lines over and over again or found that they cannot remember anything from the chapter just minutes after reading it. With difficult and complex reading, even if you read slowly and carefully, you may still get lost and the meaning of the text may elude you. The complicated language seems foreign and the ideas are so new that you may have a hard time grasping the meaning of the reading. If you've encountered a text that reads like mumbo jumbo, then gather some reinforcements before diving in.

Pick up a summary guide and preview the chapters that you plan on reading. The summary guide should not serve as a substitute for the actual book. The guide is a tool that will give you a framework for understanding the actual reading. Let us repeat again that you aren't reading the summary guide instead of the actual book. You are just clearing the pathway so that you have an idea of what you're reading. Now that you have familiarized yourself with the general idea, you can read the assigned work. As with

worksheet:
book dissection

What to do: Fill in the spaces as you complete your reading assignment.

My Guide to [   ] by [   ]

Ch. #	Summary/ Themes	Important Characters/ Events	My Questions	How I Felt Reading the Chapter

textbook reading, break it up into manageable sections and after reading each section pause to reflect on what you've read. Take a few notes before moving to the next section, or you can use the Worksheet on the previous page. Make as many copies as you need to cover all of the chapters.

Keep in Mind:

» Don't recopy the entire book.

» Use the headings and bolded words as a guide for your notes.

» Any information that was covered in class and is discussed in the textbook requires extra attention.

Those Infamous Five Paragraphs: The Essay

When we made the transition from middle to high school, it very quickly became evident that the teachers' expectations of our writing abilities had changed. It was definitely not okay if our essays contained typos or grammatical errors, be they handwritten in-class work or typed up drafts done at home. It became obvious that we were also supposed to be writing a lot more than we had previously. It was necessary to adapt to these raised standards, and fast. The following is a condensed version of the essay wisdom that was passed on to us.

A brief but necessary note here: The essay guide below should by no means be considered a complete investigation of essays and essay writing (although it seems quite full of information as is). However, when approaching any essay, there are three essential parts to getting from start to finish: Brainstorming, outlining, and drafting. Regardless of the type of essay you are tackling, these three components are absolutely crucial to get from approaching the initial question or topic, to developing a final product you are satisfied with. In the next section, we'll take you through an abridged version of an essay manual and discuss the various types of essays you may be asked to crank out. Then, we'll address how to Brainstorm your ideas; yes, in case you wondered, we definitely went through a lot of Brainstorming sessions in the course of writing this book. However, since most of our chicken scratchings mean little to anyone but us, we'll spare you from having to attempt to translate them. After we look at ways to Brainstorm, we'll talk about how to assess and organize what you've come up with. To start things off on the right foot, here's an Outline of what you'll be seeing:

Types of Essays and How to Tackle Writing an Essay

I. How Different Types of Essays Shape Your Approach
   a. Expository
   b. Narrative
   c. Persuasive

II. I Have an Essay Question/Topic . . . Now What?
   a. Step 1: Brainstorm
      i. Web Map of Ideas
      ii. Bulleted-List Form
   b. Step 2: Crafting a Thesis
   c. Step 3: Outlining Your Thoughts
   d. Step 4: Drafting
   e. Step 5: Editing
      i. Finessing Your Essay
      ii. Editing Checklist

From here, we'll take you through the actual draft-writing component of essay writing.

How Different Types of Essays
Shape Your Approach

By now, the thought of which classes you'll be using these techniques for has likely crossed your mind. It is true that an English essay is not planned out and composed in exactly the same language and format as an essay for your history class; even within your English class, you'll probably be asked to write in various styles, depending on the assignment. These differences in writing styles can be defined by the following categories: expository, narrative, and persuasive. These categories can further be grouped by voice types, such as descriptive (definition, classification and explanation included); sequential or cause/effect; reflective or compare/contrast; and evaluation or choice (opinion).

Each of these approaches to writing an essay involves a different type of analysis, from critical thinking to personal evaluation, and even to creative thinking or philosophical contemplation. The essay prompt will help you to choose the appropriate style of writing to use, but in any essay, your language should be clear, simple, and relevant. We'll take you through each style and voice you can choose from to create a successful essay.

You will probably hear the term **expository writing** with increasing frequency as you move up through grade levels, and it basically just means that the point of your essay is to explain, describe, or inform your audience on a given topic. In this type of essay, you should assume that your reader(s) have not had any previous exposure to your topic. In expository writing, try to keep your language and vocabulary clear, simple and relevant, while avoiding outright, oversimplified statements like, "This is what I mean about this" (Filling in the underlined with the appropriate topic information).

In expository writing, you'll find yourself using the techniques of: giving definitions of terms—translation, you need to say what exactly a given concept is (followed by demonstrative examples);

descriptions of what a given subject is like and what it's made up of; and classification of ideas into separate and distinct categories (also including clear examples). Similarly, you could be asked to compare and/or contrast by describing similarities and/or differences between the given topic and another topic that you've studied. A good way to set up a compare/contrast essay is to first introduce just one topic, and then compare it to another in later paragraphs. Another way to organize this type of essay is to compare subjects (or examples) through underlying categories (bigger ideas or themes). This approach makes use of your ability to think a bit more creatively by tying together certain subjects under a larger concept. History essays tend to be written in an expository form: "Could the Hiroshima tragedy have been avoided?" "What events led to the Battle of Gettysburg?" etc.

In essays voiced from a **narrative perspective,** you present a story—a clear sequence of events, either fictional or nonfictional, that occurs over a given period of time. The order in which events occur is clearly communicated from author to audience, and your aim is to describe an experience, typically including the "who, what, when, where, why, and how." You can "bring a story to life" through your descriptions of characters and settings—draw your audience into a given context by detailing how the subject looks, smells, feels, or sounds. You'll probably hear the phrase, "Show, don't tell," often enough from your teachers, but they may particularly have a point in the case of narrative essays—you can be more effective by "painting" the scene with descriptive words rather than just listing what is going on in a given place in plain language.

Often, in English, you will find that a story that you read or write has a deeper meaning, and that the story is really a means of illustrating this underlying concept. Examples of genre that use narrative writing are folktales, tall tales, fables, parables, fantasies, science fiction, plays, historical fiction and nonfiction, legends, myths, mysteries, short stories, and autobiographies. Here, you may also be given the option of something usually avoided in writing essays: You can write from a first person perspective. While this is generally a no-no for essays in history, you can often give a very compelling explanation from the "I" point of view, even if you are not necessarily the "I" describing this account. Useful techniques to incorporate into your narrative are sequential (a description of a series of events or a process in an order, chronological or otherwise, where each step of the process is written in order of occurrence), definition, description, explanation (an explanation of how or why something occurs or has occurred, outlining individual causes and effects and explaining each), and compare/contrast methods.

A **persuasive essay** is basically a strong argument that you make in which you've chosen a side. Typically, you're given a choice as to whether you are in favor of or support a given topic or statement or disagree with it, and you must take a side or particular position. The point of this type of essay is to persuade your audience to agree with you, and take on your viewpoint based on the information you present in the essay, like how a lawyer makes a case before the jury or judge she hopes to convince. In stating that there is more than one point of view (e.g., for vs. against), you also should address the position you are arguing against. This can be effective in accomplishing your goal of persuading the reader to agree with you by analyzing and pointing out flaws in the opposition's argument. Your goal should always be to convince your reader by informing him or her on the subject, and shaping your argument with solid evidence that supports your viewpoint.

A strong persuasive essay clearly defines the subject under consideration and gives the author's point of view about this subject. It is important to keep in mind to whom you are writing this argument—that is, who is the audience that will read your essay? Whether your audience is undecided or strongly opposed to your position will further influence how you shape your argument. Consider your supporting facts and figure out which one gives your argument the most weight—you'll want to present this one last in your essay so that it remains most clearly in the reader's mind. Supporting evidence for your essay's basic premise can include statistics, expert opinions, logical arguments, and even personal observations. Similarly, it can be very effective to present and take apart the strongest point of the opposing view. Techniques that are effective in achieving the aim of persuasion are the definition, description, explanation, and compare/contrast voices, supported further by causes and effects and evaluation of the material you choose to present.

Because these kinds of essays each have their own character-istics, these differences should be reflected in your Outline. This could follow a bare-bones format as presented in the previous section, but be sure your Outline targets your thesis, supporting evidence or arguments, and conclusion accordingly. However, the common thread in approaching any essay is to create a strong the-sis, or topic sentence that answers the question (we will go into detail about how to construct an effective Thesis Statement in the Draft Writing section), This is best done by thoroughly Research-ing your subject matter and evaluating which facts or examples will best support your main point. From here, it should be fairly easy to put your information together in an organized fashion so that you can build an argument. If need be, you can use the Internet to find a template to guide you in further putting together a cohesive argument, but remember that your final product must reflect your opinions, so stick to your intuition and trust your own choices about how you feel your compiled material should be presented.

I Have the Essay Question/Topic . . . Now What?

Step 1—Brainstorming. The one thing that will get you into trouble the fastest is diving headfirst into writing your essay.

Essays are structured and follow a logical thought process, so just scribbling down whatever sentences first pop into your head is likely not the most reasonable way to start this type of assignment. Instead, you'll want to jot down the initial ideas you come up with in a more manageable fashion—translation: Brainstorm your ideas before attempting to write. Often, the hardest part of writing an essay is thinking of what to write. A Brainstorm is a good way to jumpstart your brain to analyze the given topic of discussion.

The easiest way to start a flow of ideas that will gradually transform into a decipherable and logical piece is to begin with a Brainstorm. Your Brainstorm should not be screened, Edited or filtered—really, this is the place you should write down any and everything that comes to mind. There are no right or wrong answers here, so worry about clarifying and honing your ideas later. Provided that you're given an essay prompt, some additional questions to guide you in tapping into your brain are: "What is the essay question really asking?", "What do you think of when you see this _____ (word/theme/concept/idea)?", and "What material or evidence do I have that might relate to this idea?"

The way you choose to Brainstorm depends entirely on your personal preference or method of thinking (see Chapter 2). You may be a list person, whose Brainstorm may consist of a series of bullet-pointed ideas, or if you're a divergent thinker, you may choose to "web" out your ideas. This is often referred to as free association. If you tend to process things best in a visual format, it can be helpful to find symbols or pictures that show the concepts you plan to address throughout your essay. These can easily be manipulated in the Organization step to come.

Here's an example of how to approach the essay question "Discuss the changes in the relationship between Elizabeth Bennet and Mr. Darcy."

Let's take a look at an example of a Web Map of Ideas:

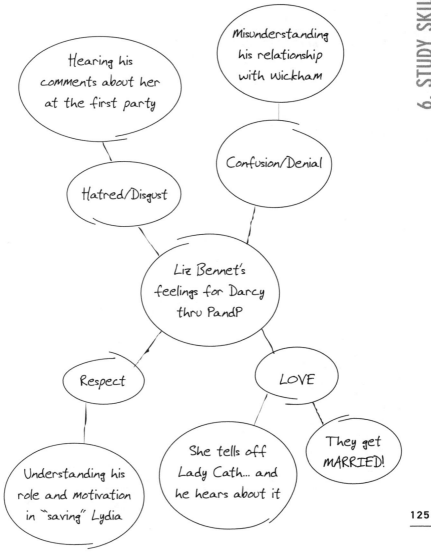

worksheet:
web map of ideas

What to do: Fill in the appropriate slots with whatever comes to mind. Also, feel free to expand with more circles if necessary.

Essay question:

If you prefer to see your thoughts in a slightly more methodical or direct train of thought fashion, here is an example of a bulleted list for the same essay question:

Essay question: How did Lizzie's feelings about Darcy change throughout *Pride and Prejudice*?

* Hate
* She heard his comments about her at the first party
* She was annoyed at his "snobbery" when he wouldn't dance
* Respect
* She understood his role in "saving" Lydia
* She saw how devoted he was to his friends and sister
* Love
* She told off Lady Catherine, and he found out about it
* They got married!!

Her feelings changed as she gradually overcame her "pride".

Step 2—Crafting a Thesis. Your *thesis statement* is the point of your essay stated in all of **one** sentence. This sentence is placed in your introduction, or thesis paragraph. It should cover three aspects: the topic, your opinion or analysis of the topic, and the ways in which you support your topic (sub-topics; these will be the main points of your body paragraphs). The two main questions you should always keep in mind while writing are, "**Why** is this important [to my point]?" and "**How** does this support and prove my point?" If you constantly ask yourself these questions, not just in terms of your sub-topics, but even in how you choose what supporting evidence to include, then you'll always stay on target and never stray from the essay's aim.

Sometimes, your essay prompt can be helpful here and can be used to create a concise thesis statement that can guide the direction your paper will take, but this is not always the case. In order to put together the most effective thesis statement that addresses your essay topic, you should gather as much information as you can get your hands on. This means sifting through your notes (class notes, book notes, homework, handouts, etc.), with a particular eye out for main points that you or your teacher emphasized in some way. These may be statements a classmate or your teacher made during class, highlighted with the obligatory, "This is a **key** point to consider." Or, it could even be an entire homework assignment you've already completed that has been considerably expanded (as we discussed earlier in the section on taking class notes). The essays you're assigned aren't just random ideas that pop into your teacher's head either. Teachers have given a great deal of thought to *what* they want you to think about, and they want to see *how* you do this. The *what* and *how* are the two most important components to your writing, which we'll go into more detail when you actually start to write.

Step 3—Outlining Your Thoughts. This is where you create an organized method for the madness. Once you've written down at least a couple of ideas that describe or relate to your assigned essay topic, it's easy to lose focus of what you're really supposed to be writing about. Since it can be difficult to filter through all of the possible paths your essay could take, it's a good idea to try to organize your thoughts so you can pick apart your core ideas from the messiness of your Brainstorm. Depending on the type of Brainstorming you've chosen, you can now start to pick and choose the more relevant ideas or concepts you want to concentrate on in your essay. You can separate these out by highlighting or circling these topics on your original list/idea map, and transferring them onto a fresh sheet of paper to see them more distinctly from the larger jumble of ideas. Now that you've narrowed your focus to target the essay topic, it's time to figure out which direction you'd like your essay to go in.

When you've gathered enough ideas and examples for support, you may be tempted once again to barrel right ahead into writing your essay: don't! While you may have crafted your thesis and even carefully selected the content of your body paragraphs, your brain is not quite ready. Now is the time to put your thoughts and information into a more coherent format, and organizing them in an Outline is one of the clearest ways to set yourself up to write.

A successful essay relies on strong supporting details to emphasize key points. Creating an Outline ensures that each of your points has the necessary support to form solid and persuasive arguments. The more details you include from the start, the better off you will be in writing the actual essay. Using an Outline is particularly helpful if you know what you want to say, but just can't find the right words. If you come up against this type of writer's block, you can turn to the Outline as a base for you to build sentences upon—just write or type out your Outline and turn your Outline points and ideas into sentences. You can always clean up your work when you go back to Edit. Just to give you an idea of how to set one up, here is an Outline template:

I. *Introduction*

    A. Thesis statement (as first or last sentence, depending on [teacher] preference)

    B. Introductory statements

    C. Introduce supporting ideas (optional)

II. *Body (You will have one to three of these, each presenting a different idea to support your thesis)*

    A. Supporting idea

    B. Transition, topic sentence

    C. Discussion, examples, and analysis

    D. Conclusion (optional)

III. *Conclusion*

    A. Transition, statement reflecting back on thesis

    B. Restate key points

    C. Ending statement that provokes thought

worksheet:
essay outline

What to do: In an essay Outline you will use your Roman numerals as paragraphs, letters as topic sentences, and numbers for details.

I. Introduction

    A. Introductory points:

        1. _____

        2. _____

        3. _____

    B. Thesis statement: _____

II. Body Paragraphs

    A. First Supporting Idea (Topic Sentence): _____

        1. _____

        2. _____

        3. _____

    B. Second Supporting Idea (Topic Sentence): _____

        1. _____

        2. _____

        3. _____

    C. Third Supporting Idea (Topic Sentence): _____

        1. _____

        2. _____

        3. _____

III. Conclusion

    1. Closing statement points

        1. _____

        2. _____

        3. _____

    2. Revisit thesis: _____

Step 4—Drafting. By now, you're well on your way to writing a strong essay, even though you haven't even begun to start writing. Coming up with ideas of what to write and then formulating a clear plan of how you want to present your material is more than half the challenge, so now that you've built your foundation, it's time to fill it in with a more complete picture. Stick to your Outline as best you can, since it too (in addition to the how and why questions) will keep you on track.

To get yourself started writing, it's often helpful to do something called a free writing session. What this means is that you sit down at your desk with your computer (or paper and pen) and your Outline to use as a reference as needed. You take note of the time, and just start writing down everything and anything that comes to mind about your topic of interest for approximately fifteen minutes without stopping. This is one of the few times when you really shouldn't be concerned with your grammar, spelling, neatness of work, or even how relevant your thoughts are—just focus on continually writing for about fifteen minutes without any breaks (in typing or writing). Content and format are things to concentrate on and refine later. Hopefully, you'll be able to continue writing, but aim for at least these first fifteen minutes of nonstop writing.

Your initial draft should consist of a strong thesis statement, with some relevant background information included in your introduction paragraph. From there, you'll put together the necessary supporting paragraphs to your thesis, making sure to state your evidence and analysis clearly as simply as possible to convey your thoughts. Be sure to keep your thesis, or main point of your essay, in mind while writing out these body paragraphs. Finally, you'll want to put together a conclusion that pulls both your thesis and supporting ideas together in a clear fashion.

How you approach writing an essay is based on your learning tendencies, and you may choose to not create a thesis statement until you've decided what evidence or information you'd like to use. You may also prefer to come up with a strong thesis before deciding how you'd like to break up your supporting facts. One way is not better than the other, nor is one right and the other wrong. However, your teacher may have his or her own preference for how you begin an essay, and you may be asked/required to hand in a draft or stand-alone thesis before proceeding with your writing.

Step 5—Editing. Now that we've overloaded you with a ton of expectations of what to put into your writing, here are some tips on what not to do. You will probably find it difficult not to repeat yourself, since you are trying to prove a specific point, particularly in your body paragraphs. In Editing your paper, you may find that you've written the same terms, sentences, or even entire analyses more than once within the same phrase or paragraph. However, do your best to try and shake things up for your reader by using different vocabulary or wording to get your point across. Similarly, filler words like "very" or "really important" and clichés like, "As you can see . . ." or, ". . . dug himself into a hole he couldn't get out of . . ." are useless and empty, so you should avoid them. These types of sentences are in the same vein as a "thesis" statement that reads, "A main theme demonstrated in this novel is love." This is too generic. There are numerous ways to describe the "love" mentioned in a novel and you need to give a clearer and more detailed statement. Any supporting statements you use to further your thesis argument are very important, so don't come out and say they are—the reader already knows they are, because you *chose* them.

Finally, try not to insert yourself into the essay with statements that read, "I believe . . ." Again, it is clear that you "believe," since you are writing on the topic so just start with the idea itself. This gives it the focus it deserves and doesn't detract from or weaken it with introductory comments that imply a certain emotional attachment or bias. The only exception to this would be if you were writing a personal narrative.

The key to successful writing is not to give up with just one shot! Brainstorming and outlining are crucial for coming up with and hashing out any ideas that you might have. Try writing on various topics, or even testing different ways of writing a single paragraph (such as your introduction). The more you practice your writing through drafting, the easier and more natural it becomes to formulate and organize your piece.

Finessing Your Essay

You're at that point where the finish line is in sight and you're ready for the final sprint. However, your brain is not actually quite ready for such physical exertion—after all, you just finished writing an entire essay! Instead, leave it be for a period of time. Understandably, if you're writing an in-class essay, the thought of taking time away from your writing might induce a mild panic, but in reality, you're better off taking a brief breather before going back in to assess your work. When your essay is a homework assignment, you have more time to work with it, and taking at least a few hours, if not an entire day or two, between writing and Editing will give you a fresh perspective you'd otherwise be cheating yourself of. (Yes, this means that writing your essay the night before it is due is not a good idea).

After distancing yourself a bit from the intense effort you've just invested, come back to the essay and put those fresh eyes to use. If you're working on this at home, print out a hard copy of your essay and go over it with a colored pen. Since you're used to seeing red ink, you may prefer to or not to write in red, but pick any color other than black (since this is what you've presumably printed in). Read over your essay carefully for its content to make sure you've said exactly what you want to say, but also keep an eye out for grammatical or typographical errors. It might be wise to read the essay over backwards, one sentence at a time, starting from your conclusion and working your way back to the introduction.

This way, you're more likely to catch any mistakes you've made, since reading through from beginning to end is how you wrote in the first place and you're more likely to see what you intended to write instead of what you've actually written down. This is also an especially useful technique when writing in-class essays. Make sure to correct your work in a differently colored pen (if you can—time constraints for in-class essays usually make this nearly impossible), make clear notes of what exactly you should amend.

Finally, it's particularly helpful to have a truly fresh set of eyes review your work, so ask your teacher, a classmate, a friend, or even a parent or sibling to read over your drafts. Ideally, you will go through the process of writing and evaluating your work more than once, creating multiple drafts of your essay. This is not an option for an in-class essay, but if your assignment is stretched over a greater length of time than one class period, try to make the most of the time you have by drafting as much as is necessary.

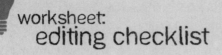

worksheet:
editing checklist

What to do: Make sure to read carefully through your essay to check for mistakes and correct them. The following is a checklist of crucial components to make sure you're set.

Grammar and Spelling

☐ Do you have any typos or misspelled words?

☐ Is all of your grammar accurate?

☐ Do all of your sentences have a subject?

☐ Do your subjects agree with your verbs?

☐ Are all of your verbs in the correct tense?

☐ Do your sentences make sense?

Style and Organization

☐ Do you have an introduction paragraph?

☐ Do you have [enough] supporting paragraphs?

☐ Do you have a conclusion?

☐ Is your thesis statement clear and answer the question?

☐ Are your paragraphs in the correct format?

☐ Do you have enough supporting evidence for each body paragraph?

☐ Do your supporting paragraphs support your thesis?

CHAPTER 7

Maintenance Work: Staying with It, Subject by Subject

For most of our academic careers, we thought that pop (or unannounced) quizzes were horrible and completely unfair. How could teachers be so cruel as to just randomly demand that we spit out information with no warning? However, we gradually realized that our teachers were actually sending us this message: This stuff is important now, so know it now! This message slowly ingrained itself into our study habits, and is what we now describe as Daily Maintenance Work.

Never mind the whole school year; in the course of just one week, you've had quite a number of new concepts introduced to you in your classes! How well you really learn and understand these concepts based on only what you were told in class varies greatly. However, by working a bit every day, you can ensure that you thoroughly comprehend all topics in great depth with minimal effort. Daily Maintenance Work refers to the little bit of extra work you need to do each day to reinforce the ideas taught by your teacher that day. From here you can build upon this base so that you continually retain all the information you learn.

What exactly we mean by Daily Maintenance Work may initially sound like extra work. However, this small bit of effort is necessary to reinforce concepts that were learned earlier. This process keeps the information you've already learned clean and well-maintained. When study time comes around you'll be a huge step ahead.

So now to clarify: What is Daily Maintenance Work? It is repetition and practical application of the concepts taught in class so they are committed to your long-term memory. Some of you may be thinking, "Wait, doesn't that just mean doing the homework assigned?" Yes and no. Homework is an assignment given to you by your teacher that absolutely must be completed; Daily Maintenance Work can be thought of as the homework you give yourself. Your teachers make sure that you complete your assignments by factoring them into your grades and penalizing you if you fail to meet these expectations. However, if you don't stick with your Daily Maintenance, your grades will suffer in a more subtle way. You'll see the effects of slacking off in your performance on quizzes, tests, and larger projects, which ultimately have a greater effect on your grades. Daily Maintenance Work allows you to solve problems more easily, efficiently, and quickly. Daily Maintenance Work will ensure that you are prepared for all manners of pop quizzes. You will never be caught off guard and feel unprepared in class!

Your Daily Maintenance Work should set up a running, subject-specific list at the end of the day of topics that were covered in each class (both reviewed and newly introduced). This list can include any problems from the previous evening's homework that you found particularly challenging or that took a long time to solve, or those questions that you answered incorrectly. It's important to keep a small spiral notebook (or separate section in a binder) for each subject in order to stay organized within each subject—this will make sure that you keep track of challenging topics to review in chronological order. This notebook should be used solely for Maintenance Work—we'll get to what a gold mine this notebook will be in the future later. We recommend that the Maintenance Workbook have a permanent place at home so that you don't lose it.

Here is how and what to do for Daily Maintenance Work of each subject.

NOTE: Although you might find this section very repetitive, do your best to look through each subject breakdown—the layout and key points to cover are similar, but the content varies widely!

Math

Typically, you should pick two to three problems from the previous night's homework that were done incorrectly and transfer them to your math Daily Maintenance notebook section so that you can be sure you can solve them correctly. If you answered all of your homework accurately, you can pick those problems that were particularly tough or tedious. Often, a teacher will mention that a particular problem from the homework was "a good question"; this tells you the question or one similar to it is a potential test question. It makes sense to copy these questions into the maintenance notebook as well. For future reference (such as finals), it's wise to keep track of all the stuff you got wrong on tests by tracking such problems in the maintenance notebook. You can later use all of the information you've entered into your maintenance book to use as study problems for unit/chapter test or even final exams. Your maintenance notebook pages are easiest to follow if laid out in this format:

1. Date the page.
2. Copy over any problems that were done incorrectly from last night's homework.
3. Select two to three problems from previous night's homework which were particularly tough (that you either got incorrect or took an exceptional amount of time to complete).

4. Pick one to two problems from two, three, four, etc. nights before. (Each day you should rewrite problems that were originally wrong or tough from all the previous nights).

5. Solve the problems and check.

6. At the end of the week create a mini-quiz with one of each type of problem from each night. If you are still having trouble solving the problems, make sure to speak to your teacher.

Use the problems in this notebook to prepare for the test.

Science

Overall, you should keep running list of key terms from class notes, textbook highlights, etc., in your maintenance notebook. These terms should also be transferred onto note cards, where the term appears on the front and the definition on the back. Also, it's a good idea to pick example problems from previous night's homework that you either got wrong or which were pointed out in class and redo them, as you did with math Maintenance. These problems can also be transferred to another running list that can be used to study for later tests. Your science Maintenance notebook pages should contain the following information.

1. Notes on the chapter you read that correspond with the topic covered in class.

2. A running list of key terms from class, your notes, the textbook, etc. (again, also to be written up on Flashcards).

3. Example problems from the preceding night's homework that you solved incorrectly or that were especially difficult, with the appropriate corrections.

4. One to two problems from work assigned on preceding nights (from two to four nights before). Each day, you should

rewrite problems that were originally wrong or difficult for you from all the previous nights' assignments.

5. Correct solutions to the problems.
6. At the end of the week, it's excellent review to create a mini-quiz of key terms and one of each type of challenging problems from each night. If you are still having trouble solving certain problems, speak to your teacher about them.

History

In this class, a constant review of previous class and book notes is crucial, especially of those concepts your teacher emphasizes in class. These topics are most likely to appear as short or long essay questions on your tests. Again, it's equally important to maintain running list of terms, important figures, and dates (most easily notated in the form of a timeline). Here are some key points to include in your history Maintenance notebook.

1. Read and take notes on the chapter that corresponds with the topic covered in class. As you read refer to your class notes and primary documents to expand your Outline.
2. Make a running list of key terms/people/dates.
3. Create a timeline of events.
4. Make Flashcards from information gathered in steps one to two.
5. Study these Flashcards for five minutes every day.

English

It's particularly important to keep vocabulary lists and make Flashcards to immediately and constantly review for your English classes, all the way through high school. Similarly, main themes, characters, or stylistic elements from assigned readings should be kept track of with lists and/or Flashcards—these notes can later be used to prepare for short or long essays, and even for your final exams. Constant review of the previous days' and weeks' class and book notes must be done so that you are best prepared for class and assignment work. It's easiest to do this by consolidating all this information in your English Maintenance notebook.

For example, if you have vocabulary lists, make Flashcards immediately—the term on the front and the back containing the definition, part of speech, and example sentence. Each day spend five minutes reviewing vocabulary.

Read over your notes from class for the day and expand on them in more detail with any examples, thoughts or opinions voiced in class (by you or your peers) that you may not have written down at the time.

Foreign Language

As you've likely noticed, it's absolutely essential to create vocabulary lists and make Flashcards immediately for constant review, but especially with regard to foreign language studies. Similarly with English Maintenance, it's also important to make notes or Flashcards of verb conjugations and grammar rules to constantly review. Here's a short list of necessities to include in your foreign language Maintenance book.

1. Create vocabulary lists of new words.
2. Make Flashcards from vocabulary lists.
3. Maintain separate lists of conjugation and grammar rules.
4. Remember to practice spelling!
5. Study Flashcards five minutes each day.

carolina

Carolina was voted "Most Overbooked and Underslept" in last year's tenth grade yearbook. Her best friends' nickname for her is "Captain MIA," as she rarely is able to socialize since she's busy being president of the recycling club; co-captain of the varsity soccer, club hockey, and tennis teams; stage manager for all school productions; and coach to the neighborhood's pee-wee soccer team. Her friends teasingly respond to her Facebook profile and photo posts, describing her as being "adorable," "Oh, look, another opinionated point she's making," and the "smartypants ;oP" who loves hanging out with her friends, having an awesome time playing soccer at the beach, but "never actually has the time to do ANYTHING!!" Meanwhile, her brother Jake relishes posting his own candids of his older sister, catching the family's Golden Child, at her finest moments, typically before she's even managed to fully open her eyes. Such posts typically lead to a tag war between the siblings.

Carolina's typical day starts around 5:45 A.M., when she groggily finishes whatever remaining homework assignments she needs to complete before dashing off to school to fly through her hectic schedule, rushing to hockey practice, promptly after which she runs to her various weekly club meetings, finally dragging herself home to complete her chores, check in with her increasingly studious brother, and work through as much school and SAT work as she can before conking out, only to wake the next morning to start all over again. . . .

While some of her classmates carefully write out the day's math assignments in their planners and the teacher wraps up class, Carolina fights off her dozing (likely attributed to the previous night's intense SAT study session with some friends that ran late) at the end of her last class. She jolts upright when she notices that the rest of the class has already started packing up and the teacher has left the classroom. Hurriedly, Carolina grabs her agenda book, jots down the evening's assignments, and quickly pack her bag. As she exits the classroom, she hears her friends yelling for her to meet them at the usual table at their favorite diner before hockey practice. Slightly disoriented and preoccupied, Carolina yells back that she'll catch up with them in five minutes, as she's realized that she hasn't completed her vocabulary assignment for her SAT class due immediately following practice.

Several hours later, an exhausted and fretful Carolina bursts through the front door of her house, tiredly dropping her hockey gear and gym bag in the front hallway as she trudges upstairs to her room with her backpack. After unloading her overstuffed school bag and grabbing a quick shower, she finally makes her way to the kitchen, because she's famished. While scarfing down some leftover veggie pizza, her mind repeatedly drills through her assignments and projects as if on autopilot, until she realizes that she's eaten all of the leftover pizza. Carolina stands abruptly, overwhelmed by waves of anxiety and the sensation of being on the verge of physically exploding. A note from her guidance counselor begins to float to the front her mind. "Carolina, I'm concerned that you're not taking enough time to fully dedicate yourself to the many commitments you've taken on. I would suggest that, at least for your academic work, you try to implement a more methodical routine. I don't want you to fall behind or get too overwhelmed. Please come see me any time to discuss this further."

When she first got this note, Carolina had cocked an eyebrow and merely tucked the note into her pocket. Now, as she feels fully the weight of all of her responsibilities, she realizes her counselor actually may have a good point. She silently acknowledges that she has been getting by with most of her day-to-day work, but that she's finding it increasingly difficult to prepare for her exams. Her history teacher poses a particular challenge because he constantly says that students must know every nuance of historical information. His history exams are notoriously rigorous and difficult, demanding an extensive and thorough grasp of details. In preparing for the first test of the year, Carolina quickly realized that she had grossly underestimated the amount of information that she was expected to know, as she frantically reviewed unending lists of dates, names, and battles the preceding night. Needless to say, her resulting grade didn't hide her lack of preparedness, not to mention her intense disappointment with her performance and poor planning.

Other than the year's history tests, Carolina also worries about her math class. While she enjoys the class and has always liked the "one-right-answer clarity" of mathematics, she feels a particular importance about this year's course, as her final grade will determine whether or not she will qualify for twelfth grade AP Calculus. Next year, she knows, the AP Calc class will be taught by Carolina's favorite math teacher, and Carolina has promised herself to win a seat in the class. As a result, she is resolved to maintain at least a 92 percent average and not miss any more than one homework assignment.

Overcoming her current agitation, Carolina decides to face the expectations she has set for herself and dedicate the remaining few hours of her evening to getting ahead in her math and history work. Of course, with her keen interest in math, she tackles that subject first. She decides to recopy any problems from the previous night's homework that she had marked as wrong in class to her math Daily Maintenance notebook, for future use as practice examples in studying for tests. Upon reviewing her week's assignments, she realizes that she did not get many problems wrong. Feeling suddenly confident, Carolina is about to end her math work when she thinks back to a few particularly challenging homework problems. While she finally figured out how to solve these difficult questions, she now recalls they were very time-consuming and draining, and decides to revisit these problems. Besides, she notes to herself, keeping a list of the hard questions is really helpful for when test time does finally come around. She flips to a blank page in her math maintenance notebook and spends the next ten minutes noting down and redo-ing select problems.

Once she completes her math Daily Maintenance exercises, she moves on to deal with her history assignments. Carolina vaguely remembers what new material was covered in class over the course of the week, and sighs as she begins to read the textbook pages her teacher had mentioned as being helpful, and takes thorough book notes on the information. She glosses over the text, noting titles, sub-headings, and bolded words, recording the highlighted key words and their definitions in her notebook. Once she finishes her overview of the pages, Carolina pleasantly realizes that she is only required to read about five pages, which didn't take as long to slog through as she'd expected. She then reads the passages in depth for content and detail, marking several key themes in the reading to review again later. Afterward, she examines her notes, transferring important facts (dates, people, events, etc.) onto Flashcards, even though she's so tired she can barely keep her eyes open. Relieved and pleased with her progress, she decides to finish the remaining Flashcards the next morning to study on the way to school.

Carolina surveys her work and grins to herself, feeling more at ease and prepared for the next day's classes. Before going to bed, Carolina opens her planner and glances through it, searching for time slots during the week when she can continue her new history and math review exercises. While it may be impossible to devote time to Daily Maintenance Work every day, she figures that she might manage extra review on the days when she's able to return home earlier. Carolina takes out her favorite blue highlighter and selects time blocks on Mondays, Wednesdays, Thursdays, and Sun-days for math and history Daily Maintenance Work, relieved at the thought of how much more sleep she'll be getting the nights before any future math or history exams. Sleepily, she packs up her school bag and glances at her bedside alarm clock, and realizes that she can flip through her favorite fashion magazine before going to bed.

CHAPTER 8

Talking to Your Teachers

Many students do not feel comfortable approaching a teacher to talk one-on-one. Okay, you might even be down-right scared. This is quite understandable since teachers are often seen as just being the imposing figures at the front of a classroom. Teachers seem to be capable of doing anything from solving the most complicated of math problems to speaking at length about the most detailed parts of a given subject. They seem to know every tidbit of information a given textbook contains, and to many students, they can come across as being difficult to understand, let alone to talk to. However, forming a workable (if not enjoyable) relationship with your teacher is an important and necessary step in your learning process.

Despite any impression you may have formed to the contrary, no teacher actually wants his students to fail. In fact, the truth is quite the opposite—your teachers really are interested and invested in your academic success. After all, they have dedicated themselves to knowing and teaching a particular subject to you and your peers, so it's not as if they are purposely torturing you with challenging homework or tests. They really want to see that you are gaining something from their hard work. (Yes, teachers do have to work outside of the classroom to make sure that you're actually getting something out of their teaching). So, to hold up your end of the deal, a little effort to show them that you care about learning what they teach and are committed to your studies can go a long way.

Even if you already have a previously established relationship with your teacher through an older sibling, an extracurricular activity, or a previous year of school, striking up conversation or popping in with a question can still be hard, but it really is worth your while to try. Your teachers do know a lot of stuff and often turn out to be very interesting people. Just by spending even a little outside-of-class time talking with your teacher, you may discover something new about your own academic interests or find a new way to think about a concept or subject.

Signs of an S.O.S.: When to Make the Meeting

Even though they might seem a bit intimidating or even strange, your teachers are a resource you should make the most of. There may be a time or two (or even more often) when you may be sitting in class, feeling slightly (or more) shaky on a concept being presented, or maybe something isn't made clear enough to you in the larger group setting of class time. This is an example of when you should see your teacher so that she can explain what was taught in class. You should most definitely seek help outside of class if you are starting to feel overwhelmed by the quick pace at which your teacher is covering material.

While this may seem like a painful suggestion, introduce yourself to your teachers at the start of each school year. (Yes, again, this may be an incredibly socially awkward moment for you, but you'll survive, really). Introducing yourself is a polite and friendly gesture that your teachers will remember, and let's be honest: Making a good first impression never hurts. What is not an equally bright idea is to wait until six months have passed and you realize that you've no idea as to what on earth is going on in any given class, and then show up unannounced at your teacher's office door with nothing more than a blank stare to offer. Yes, your teacher is there to help you, but no teacher can miraculously re-teach you in a short period of time in what they've already spent an entire six months covering.

In the same vein, it is not a good idea to appear at your teacher's desk days (or worse, hours) before an important test or a big project due date. This isn't just an unfair (and fairly rude) move, but you're not giving your brain the time it needs to learn or produce large volumes of work on short notice. Make the first move and try to schedule appointments with your teacher in advance to prevent from having to deal with "crunch time" panic. This will give you (and your brain) the relief of knowing that your teacher has a heads-up about your problem and is likely to be more than willing to help.

While your teacher may offer study halls, office hours, or review sessions, you should think about meeting with her separately in addition to these particular opportunities to talk. This might help you feel less uncomfortable about asking for help (if you're nervous about doing so to start with), and it also gives your teacher a chance to see you outside the context of class. This independent meeting allows for your teacher to think of you as You, as opposed to "that guy in the third row who always wears that baseball hat." When you establish this personal relationship, your teacher is more likely to make time to meet with you. If you feel like you're particularly struggling with a given class, consider making a weekly appointment with your teacher for that class. You'll be in a much better position to keep up with the class and constantly review particularly challenging material. As most classes are fairly cumulative, this additional weekly help-session is the best way for you to be more prepared for anything your teacher presents you with, tests, papers, exams, and the like.

Meeting with your teachers during free periods or after school gives you an excellent opportunity to review trouble spots and ask questions that matter or help with your understanding of given material. Seeing your teacher at a separate, out-of-class time that works for both of you lets you ask about whatever topics you might be feeling less than comfortable with. These could be just basic questions about information you received in class or much more specific questions regarding your homework or a graded assignment. If ever you've walked out of a test feeling like you not only studied well and hard, but that the work you did was actually enough to earn you that awesome grade you deserve, and were seriously disappointed with a grade below what you expected, see your teacher. This way, you can find out why you got the grade that you did instead of guessing at how your teacher arrived at such an assessment. It could be that certain aspects of your studying were right on the mark, but you didn't apply what you learned accurately in the context of certain questions. The only person who can truly give you the answer would be the one who gave you the grade, your teacher.

Your teachers can help you see what went wrong and help you improve, especially when it comes to homework, tests, essays, or any assignments for which you feel you were penalized unfairly. Meeting one-on-one allows your teacher to pinpoint what your weaknesses are for you; no one likes hearing about what he is not that good at. But it's still a necessary step to getting where you want to be. You can make a very favorable impression just by having a meeting to review such an assignment because it shows your teacher how personally invested in your studies you really are. More importantly, your teacher gets the chance to see exactly how you've digested what she's taught you, and let you know how accurately you have done so. By getting an idea of how you learn (which is most effectively done in a face-to-face setting), your teacher can adjust how she explains material to make it more understandable in your language. You may even find that your information and understanding is completely accurate, but your teacher may want you to present it differently, and she can tell what you can do to meet her expectations.

As odd or clichéd as it may sound, it really does make your and your teachers' lives a lot easier when you open this route of communication, since teachers really are just human beings. Meeting with your teachers can only reinforce any positive opinion they may already have of you since you are expressing an interest in the very subject and passion to which they've chosen to dedicate their career.

Umm, Excuse Me, Professor: How to "Do" the Meeting

Now that we've explored the benefits of talking to your teachers (and hopefully convinced you of how very useful an endeavor it really is), let's turn our attention to how to actually begin the conversation.

Once you've scheduled a meeting at a time that's mutually convenient for you and your teacher, you will need to prepare for the meeting. Remember that you are seeing your teacher both to get help or clarity on a topic and to show him that you take your learning process seriously. An important point to keep in mind is that your teachers are busy individuals who take their work seriously, and by extension, hope that you do too. This means that your teachers actually do expect you to hold up your end of the bargain as a student, since they also have the rest of an entire class (or classes) to teach as well.

To make the most of the meeting time, come as prepared as possible. Make sure to bring any notes or written questions, especially if there are things that you didn't understand in class or in your homework. In order to maintain the good impression you've made thus far, be sure that your materials are orderly; showing up with a binder stuffed with random, irrelevant papers and any incomplete work (homework or unfinished assignments of any kind) will undermine the very effort you're making by meeting.

Your teacher will want to see that you've done as much as you can on your own to try and resolve your confusion, and that you aren't just showing up for a review because you were too busy passing notes to your friend during class. In these cases, the more concrete efforts you can show your teacher, the easier it becomes to resolve areas that are unclear to you, since your notes will likely show where the problem is.

However, there may be times when you feel absolutely lost in class and are too paralyzed to meet with the teacher. You may have let things slide for that particular class and didn't go to the teacher for help to get back on track early enough, or perhaps you got absolutely lost within the space of a single class period that you feel so overwhelmed you can't put together any specific questions. You might have the urge to come to your teacher empty-handed, hoping that he'll be able to mind-read and know exactly where you're having trouble. You might even feel embarrassed about your situation and may not want the teacher to know how confused you are. In reality, at the precise moment your teacher assesses the look of utter confusion and asks, "So, do you have any questions," you fear that on hearing your reply of, "No . . . ," he'll figure that you simply weren't listening in class and now want him to re-teach you an entire section of the material. While it might feel somewhat less than productive, you should still attend a meeting with your teacher, prepared with your notes and completed homework. Remember that your teacher is there to help you, and that the more stuff you can offer to your teacher, the more help your teacher can give you. The most important thing in the "I'm totally lost" state is to show up with proof that you've tried and still have difficulty with the given material. Review your homework and notes. Try to find when and where things got fuzzy or when your notes started to take the form of a foreign language. Is there a homework assignment that has a lot of incorrect answers or question marks? Did you start leaving out parts of your notes? Show this to your teacher and ask that she review those topics with you. Then go home, re-do your homework (think Daily Maintenance Work) and make another appointment with your teacher. The follow-up will be important both in reinforcing the information for you and also showing your teacher your commitment to learning the material.

Once you've scheduled a meeting and taken all the necessary steps to prepare for it, here are some final pointers to keep in mind for the meeting itself. First, show up on time. This sounds like a no-brainer but seriously, you don't want to show up late. This is especially true if you're seeing your teacher after school; you may get caught up in chatting with your friends or finishing the last bit of work from study hall, but don't give your teacher cause to regret (or resent) having made an extra meeting time—teachers have other things to do, like go home.

As your teacher reviews the material with you or goes over your homework problems, make sure to write down some notes (so be sure to bring along the appropriate utensils, i.e., pen, paper, calculator, etc.). These notes will be helpful when you're reviewing the material and will also show your teacher that you're engaged and participating in the meeting. Don't just sit silently while your teacher goes over the assignments. Ask questions, especially if you feel yourself getting confused. If you've let your teacher ramble on without stopping at points where you start feeling lost, the meeting loses its purpose: to un-confuse you! At the end of the meeting, make sure to thank your teacher and to schedule a follow-up meeting. If you're having trouble in the class, then consistent meetings are the best method to staying on top of your work.

bianca

This year, Bianca has encountered one of the toughest (and greatest) teachers she'll meet in all of her high school classes, although she doesn't know this at the start of the year. Typically, Mrs. Adams (better known to the underclassmen as "the Dragon Lady,") teaches the higher-level history courses, but for the past few years, she has instructed the first year high school students' classes. Nothing is more irksome to Mrs. Adams than slovenly presentation or work, a fact she makes quite clear on a regular basis. Nothing escapes this teacher's notice, and she delivers what she deems appropriate feedback in a sharp, no-nonsense tone, about the appropriateness of a student's attire for school to another's essay writing.

Mrs. Adams has been notorious for doling out C grades like candy to eighth graders at Bianca's school for as long as she's taught history there. The first year of high school is the first time the grading schema for social studies class includes things other than multiple choice tests. The new formats include short answer questions, figure or quote IDs, and essays. Despite this fact, Mrs. Adams grades these new formats the ninth graders are introduced to as if they should already be able to present solid, A-quality pieces without any practice. What is most irksome and puzzling to Bianca is the fact that this Dragon Lady is somehow adored by the students she has already had. Clearly, Bianca thinks to herself that there must be something she's missed or that was being kept secret from the students of her grade by the upperclassmen.

Within the first class period Bianca has with her, Mrs. Adams more than lives up to her reputation for being an incredibly demanding teacher by administering a pop quiz, reviewing material from the previous year. Even now well into the year, it seems like she's constantly picking on her students in class to speak, to read out their writing, or to give an opinion on the previous night's homework (probably to make sure everyone had done it), only to bombard them with unsolicited feedback about what they missed. However, Bianca is optimistic that she'll be able to dodge the C bullet that seems to strike the majority of Mrs. Adams's ninth graders. She's an incredibly hard-working and diligent student, who makes sure to finish all of her reading and homework assignments and takes good notes in class and at home.

Making sure to check the mail each afternoon for her first term's report card before her parents do, Bianca manages to be the first to view her report card, and is unpleasantly greeted by a C in Mrs. Adams's class. She'd never brag about it aloud, but Bianca had gotten used to seeing the first two letters of the alphabet on her report card, and this new unwelcome addition to her collection of grades is upsetting.

After dodging her parents' realization for about a week that the first term grades have been sent out, Bianca shamefacedly and sadly hands over the report to her mildly amused mother, waiting for the inevitable response. Surprisingly, although she blinks noticeably over the report card and slightly wrinkles her forehead at the center of the page (where Bianca knows that awful letter is glaring back), Bianca's mom calmly sits down at the kitchen counter and glances up at her, saying, "Well, what do you think?"

Bianca is silent, shocked that smoke isn't spewing out of her mom's ears. She has no idea what her mom means, and is totally disconcerted by her almost satisfied tone of voice. Clearly, Bianca's mom gathers as much since she continues, "If you're wondering, your history grade is just what we were expecting. Your middle school teachers told us this was a possible first term grade for any student transitioning from middle to high school, especially with this teacher. So now, what are you going to do about it?"

Again, Bianca has no response. She actually, truly has no idea. What is she supposed to do, apart from whining and groaning about her injured GPA to her friends, and magically finding even more time to dedicate to her history studies?

Bianca's mother gives this advice, "Why don't you go and ask your teacher what you can do to improve your work? This grade doesn't mean that you're not smart or that you're bad at history; it just means you don't know how to study."

For this comment however, Bianca definitely has a response, and exclaims, "Yes I do!! Look at my grades! What do you mean, 'I don't know how to study??'"

Her mom calmly tilts her head and says, "Well, this history grade says to me that you don't know how to study for history. It doesn't say anything about your other classes, so there must be something different about the way you should be studying for this class than the other classes." With that, Bianca's mom sets the grades down on the counter and leaves the kitchen. Still reeling ("She wasn't even mad???"), Bianca slowly gathers up her report and shuffles back to her room to plod distractedly through her evening's homework.

Later that week, Mrs. Adams brings up the report cards in class. She only has one comment, "Well, you all did better than I expected at the start of the year—good work, keep it up."

Bianca is only able to think one thing for the remainder of class: "WHAT??? This woman is completely nuts." She is certainly not the only one to have this reaction. Later, at lunch, Bianca and her friends yell in confusion. Bianca remains utterly baffled about Mrs. Adams's comments for the rest of the day. However, she begins to absorb that this is a different ballgame than her previous years' experience with history class. It truly takes personal experience with one of Mrs. Adams' essay assignments and grading to really get what it's like, and not just hear about it repeatedly and from various conduits.

Bianca finally manages to recoup once the school day is over and she's had the benefit of venting some of her frustration on the basketball court at the team's scheduled match against a rival school. She decides to set up a meeting with Mrs. Adams to see what that Dragon woman has to say about her work, and throws herself into completing her homework in record time. The next day, in a surprisingly brief and easy exchange after class, Bianca schedules her meeting with Mrs. Adams for the lunch period on Thursday later that week. However, as Thursday draws closer, Bianca's initial curiosity has quickly snowballed into nervousness and worry at being trapped in a small office with no one but Mrs. Adams.

At the lunch period time on Thursday, Bianca promptly appears in the history office doorway, and peers past the door frame, hoping not to find the person she is looking for. The Dragon Lady barely looks up and beckons her to enter and have a seat next to her at her desk. Bianca hesitantly fumbles through her papers for the appropriate essay, notes, and Outline she created prior to doing in the assignment. Mrs. Adams thoroughly examines the documents Bianca has presented, nodding periodically.

Finally, she looks up and says, "You do a good job with preparing for tests, Bianca, I can see that. You have a very good understanding of the material, and this shows in your multiple choice answers. The problem I see here is that you don't have a thesis. Walk me through your essay." By now, wholly frightened and on the verge of tears, Bianca tries to sputter about how she tried to answer the essay question by using the facts she knew, when Mrs. Adams interrupts her again. "I know that you know the material, but the problem here is in the thesis, as I said. While you think you are answering the question, you haven't addressed it at all. Here, take this book, and after you've read it, I want you to re-read your essay. Once you've done this, we will meet again."

Feeling her control over her crying slipping away, Bianca hurriedly piles her materials back into her bag, and quickly ducks out of the office to the safety of the nearest bathroom.

"She's evil!! She's a horrible person!! How could she even say that I have no thesis??? On top of that, she might as well have just told me to rewrite the stupid thing for fun!!" The end of lunch is noisily announced by the bell as Bianca wipes her eyes and hauls her bag up to trudge back to class.

That evening, Bianca stares morosely at the assigned math problems for twenty minutes before digging through her bag for the small book Mrs. Adams had put firmly in her hands on top of her essay. She flips through the pages of this tiny booklet, and slowly sits more upright in her chair as she realizes that the chapter titles and subheadings are aimed at what not to write in an essay. The whole paperback consists of fewer than a hundred pages, and Bianca zips through it in less than an hour. The rules of essay writing are stated in the clearest and most concise fashion possible. She closes the small book and reads through her essay, searching for those don'ts and is disappointed to see many, not to mention that she now reads her rewording of the essay question as a thesis statement as being completely off topic.

After class the next day, Bianca slowly makes her way to Mrs. Adams and hands the book back, saying, "Thanks for letting me borrow this. It was really helpful in showing me how bad my writing is."

Somewhat mortified that she let slip such a statement, Bianca is surprised by Mrs. Adams bursting into laughter. "Bianca, your writing is fine, you just need a bit of practice in focusing your ideas."

Mrs. Adams smiles at the still incredulous Bianca. "To be honest, you continue to impress me with your determination to improve. I didn't even expect you to be able to get to the book for another week with all the other assignments you've got!"

For the next few minutes, Mrs. Adams points out the stronger areas of her essay, laughing occasionally when Bianca can't contain her grunts of disbelief or sighs heavily at the weaker points of her writing. Although the meeting lasts less than ten minutes, Bianca leaves the Dragon's classroom feeling less disgruntled and more optimistic about her writing skills.

Over the course of the next term, Bianca continues to meet with Mrs. Adams before and after each essay and test, reviewing together the prep work Bianca completes and discussing her work in greater depth and detail. Although frustratingly slowly, Bianca finally begins to see her work with Mrs. Adams translate effectively into the increasing grades she receives. Her final grade for the second term is a B+, which she and her parents celebrate by going to dinner at her favorite restaurant. The stigma Bianca once felt for those students who had to meet with their teachers has long evaporated by the end of the year, and Bianca starts to genuinely look forward to the next year when she gets to tackle European history with her favorite Dragon Lady teacher.

PART IV:

TEST-TAKING TIPS AND TRICKS

WAYS TO ACE THE EXAM

I will study and get ready and perhaps
my chance will come.

—Abraham Lincoln

CHAPTER 9

The Study Devices to Make It All Stick

Learning is a process. Before you even try to make information actually stick, you need to first be certain that you understand the material you're trying to commit to memory. Even though we all learn in vastly different and unique ways, being able to obtain and retain information and then being able to recall it in a test setting can be very difficult and somewhat stressful for anyone. Our goal in this section is to give you the Tools to be able to understand the material enough that you could explain accurately and thoroughly it if we woke you up in the middle of the night (yeah, you'll be sleepy and possibly somewhat incoherent, but still manage to mumble the correct answers), or better still, to be able to teach it to someone else.

In the following chapters we'll take you through detailed explanations of the various Study Devices that will make information easier to memorize. Since everybody learns in different ways, it makes sense that a study strategy that is effective for one student studying math, for example, may not work for another student studying history. After this review of various Study Devices that you can apply to whatever subject you feel comfortable, we'll go into how to use these Devices to further strengthen your command of the material. It's smart to try using both approaches to make the best use of these Study Devices, so that you'll have an ease with the material that is extremely helpful in test situations.

After going through the Devices and bigger picture study techniques, we'll be ready to confront the dreaded "monsters" of tests, and guide you through the best tactics to defeat them. To make our Taming of the Test Monster more targeted, we will also discuss how to apply various Study Devices and study steps to best prepare for tests in a given subject. Finally, since our goal is to help you become the best possible student you are able to be, we'll discuss the essential factor for improvement that so few students do or are even aware of: an accurate (and fair) assessment your performance.

A Brief Review

In the previous chapter we mentioned that before you sit down to memorize or get information in your head, you will need to gather and organize your materials and plan your study time out. However, if you've forgotten (or "accidentally" skipped over it), then here's a brief recap of the main points:

» **Allocate time.** Dedicate two to ten days to your "prep time."
» **Talk to your teacher.** Ask your teacher what he or she will include on the test and what kind of format you should expect (if he or she hasn't described it or you aren't sure).
» **Revisit past exams.** Take out your old tests and examine them for types of questions, depth of questions, and length of the exam.
» **Hunt for clues.** Go through all of the notes and homework assignments that you've gotten since your last test. In your review of these materials, look out for the important concepts focused on, as notated from the old work, as these will probably reappear on the test.

» More specifically, pay particular attention to: themes that have come up in previous chapters, homework headings, concepts or problems your teacher revisited and/or spent a lot of time on, "do-now" or in-class practice problems your teacher assigns, information on the board your teacher has taken time to write out, and questions the teacher asked during class.

» **Plan time.** Decide how much time you will spend on each topic that will be tested. Write in your calendar (Worksheet: What I Know) what concepts you plan to address each day.

Now that you are familiar with the exam content and have planned out your study time, let's tackle the actual studying. As with Daily Maintenance Work, we'll first introduce and discuss various Study Devices such as Repetition, Flashcards, and Mock Tests. You may already be familiar with some of the Study Devices we talk about, but take the time to (re-)familiarize yourself with these approaches, focusing on those you have not previously used or encountered because applying these new or different Devices may improve your study process. Remember, several Devices can be combined within one study process, and various Devices can apply to any of your subjects. Again, some of these Devices will work better for you than others. It really depends on the type of learner you are. Above all, remember: The most important use of these Devices to make information really stick in your long term memory is Rehearsal and Repetition.

Meet Acronyms

Acronym seems like a weird term for something you encounter every day. An Acronym is an abbreviation of several words or terms, using the first letter of each to piece together a nonsensical word.

Daily examples that you probably use are: lol, omg, gtg, brb, ATM, AM/PM, EST/MST/PST, USA, OJ, ID, MO, IQ, PC, TBA, RSVP, PDA, PS, PMS, etc. Many of these examples have different meanings that are dependent on context, such as PDA ("public displays of affection" vs. "personal digital assistant"). In your studies, an Acronym is the word you form from the first letter of each fact to be remembered, in an order of your choosing. It can be a real word or a gibberish word you are able to pronounce and remember easily.

Steps to Creating an Acronym

Step 1: Write the facts/words you need to remember.

Step 2: Underline the first letter of each fact.

Step 3: Arrange the letters to form a real or nonsense word.

Let's say that you need to remember the names of the Great Lakes. You can either try to drill the names into your head, or you can create a memorable Acronym for yourself. Let's look at the steps together for this example:

Step 1: Write the facts
Michigan, Erie, Superior, Ontario, Huron

Step 2: Underline the first letter
Michigan, Erie, Superior, Ontario, Huron

Step 3: Arrange the letters to form a word
HOMES

Meet Acrostics (Forward and Backward)

While an Acronym is a word formed from individual facts or pieces of data, an Acrostic is slightly different. An Acrostic is a word or sentence that is formed based on data in a given order. (For you math buffs out there, the difference between an Acronym and an Acrostic is similar to the difference between using a permutation or combination calculation in a probability question: the order of facts or information matters.) There are two types of Acrostic, forward and backward, which are particularly useful for memorizing larger chunks of data in a particular order. A good Acrostic is one that is created from a silly, made-up word or nonsense combination of words.

Forward Acrostic: A word that is created using the first letter(s) of the first or last word(s) of a sentence within a larger context, such as a poem or speech.

Backward Acrostic: A sentence that is formed from the first letters of the words or facts to be memorized.

Steps to Creating a Forward Acrostic

Step 1: Write out the section of material you need to remember.

Step 2: Underline the first letter of the first or last word of each sentence.

Step 3: Using these letters in the given order, think of words that form a nonsense sentence of your own.

Let's revisit some biology for another example. Here's a short one, focusing only on the order in which things come:

Step 1: Write out the words/facts you need to remember.

Phases of Cell Division = Mitosis:

Prophase → Metaphase → Anaphase → Telophase (+ Cytokinesis)

Step 2: Underline the first (or last) letter of each word in appropriate order.

<u>P</u>rophase
<u>M</u>etaphase
<u>A</u>naphase
<u>T</u>elophase (+ Cytokinesis)

If you've ever encountered a standardized test (such as a PSAT, ISEE, SSAT, (and later) SAT, ACT, GRE), this example is particularly memorable. So, in looking at the first letters of each phase, you can create an Acrostic "PMAT."

Here is an example for longer sentences:

Step 1: Write out the words/facts you need to remember.

The beginning of the prologue from Shakespeare's Romeo and Juliet:

Two households, both alike in dignity,

In fair Verona, where we lay our scene,

From ancient grudge break to new mutiny,

Where civil blood makes civil hands unclean.

From forth the fatal loins of these two foes

A pair of star-cross'd lovers take their life;

Whose misadventured piteous overthrows

Do with their death bury their parents' strife.

Step 2: Underline the first (or last) letter of the first (or last) word of each sentence.

<u>T</u>wo households, both alike in dignity,

<u>I</u>n fair Verona, where we lay our scene,

<u>F</u>rom ancient grudge break to new mutiny,

<u>W</u>here civil blood makes civil hands unclean.

<u>F</u>rom forth the fatal loins of these two foes

<u>A</u> pair of star-cross'd lovers take their life;

<u>W</u>hose misadventured piteous overthrows

<u>D</u>o with their death bury their parents' strife.

This technique allows you to choose the first or last letter of the first or last word, but regardless of which letter you choose, try to stick with only the first letters of the first word, or the first letters of the last word, etc. This will ensure that you won't get confused about with what word the relevant line to remember either starts or ends.

Step 3: Piece together the letters to form a word (or words) that's "rememberable," based on the order in which the lines are arranged. This example is similar to "ROY G. BIV" Acrostic (for the order of light waves of the electromagnetic spectrum):

169

TIF W. FAWD

However, if you prefer to separate the letters further to remind yourself that they represent separate lines, here's another example in sentence format (this is more a backwards Acrostic, which we'll go over next):

> Tango-ers In France Wind Farts At Wimpy Ducks

The word or sentence itself is completely irrational, but is (hopefully) weird enough for you to easily recall. This study device is particularly helpful to those students who are able to memorize larger sections of information, but have a more difficult time retaining the particular order in which the information should appear.

Steps to Creating a Backwards Acrostic
Step 1: Write out the section of material you need to remember.
Step 2: Underline the first letter of each word.
Step 3: Think of words that form a memorable sentence in the appropriate order.

A typical Acrostic is one that is created from a silly combination of words. Here is an example:

Step 1: Write out the words/facts you need to remember.

> Order of operations

Step 2: Underline the first letter of each word.

> Parenthesis | Exponents | Multiplication | Division | Addition | Subtraction

Step 3: Think of words that form a memorable sentence.

> Please Excuse My Dear Aunt Sally

Meet Story Format

You know all of those fables and fairy tales you heard or read when you were younger? Stories such as *Cinderella, Hansel and Gretel,* and *The Tortoise and the Hare* come in handy when you mold words or facts into a story. Of course, it may be more effective for you to make up an entirely unique story, provided the data you need to know is organized fittingly. The Story Format Device is also especially useful when facts need to be memorized in order, as with Acrostics.

Steps to Using the Story Format
Step 1: Write out the words/facts you need to remember.
Step 2: Create a story that you can easily remember and insert the words that you are memorizing.

Often, you'll have to become familiar with words that sound completely foreign. Here's an example of how to put an unfamiliar word into an unforgettable story.

Step 1: Write out the words/facts you need to remember.

> Mitochondria

Step 2: Create a story that you can easily remember and insert the word you are memorizing.

> Mitochondria were the most energetic part of the cell and by far the strongest. Often, they were found working out at the gym or running on the track. In fact, they were so strong that the other members of the cell started calling them Mighty Mitochondria.

Meet Associations

An association is a device that sounds exactly like what it is: You link a recognizable or understandable concept you know well with a different, foreign term or idea. It's easiest to create an association between facts that need to be memorized and other words or things that you already know. Associations should be personal and formed on the basis of something that links words or facts that are well-known to your mind, like your favorite cartoon character or an action you do frequently (like eating or watching TV).

Steps to Creating Associations
Step 1: Write down the words/facts that you need to memorize.
Step 2: Think of another word or phrase that you associate with the information you are trying to memorize.

We'll show you an example here, but remember that it is something that makes sense to us but may not be as obvious to you:

Step 1: Write down the words/facts that you need to memorize.

> Define lassitude

Step 2: Think of another word or phrase that you associate with the information you are trying to memorize.

> Lassie the dog was tired after saving yet another child.

(Hint: Lassie sounds like lassitude. Yeah, we figured you'd get it pretty quickly.)

Meet Sing It

Ever notice how you're almost always able to recite the lyrics the most recent release by your favorite artist, but have a really tough time remembering math formulas or history dates and names? With Sing It, you take a song, any song—it can be a pop song, your favorite song, or even compose your own song—and make up your own lyrics. The more nonsensical they are, the more memorable they are and the more likely you are to remember their meaning in a test setting. This technique is particularly useful for those of you who dislike or don't find drills or rote memorization helpful but are good at remembering lyrics to songs.

Steps to Singing It
Step 1: Write down the words/facts you need to memorize.
Step 2: Pick a song that you know well, and put your own "lyrics" to it by inserting the facts that you need to memorize.

173

Here's an example of an old favorite:

Step 1: Write down the words/facts that you need to memorize.

> The U.S. team of the first spacewalk

Step 2: Pick a song that you know well, and put your own "lyrics" to it by inserting the facts that you need to memorize.

> To the tune of "On Top of Spaghetti":
>
> "Apollo Eleven
> Took off into space
> Collins, Aldrin, Armstrong
> Won the first Space Race"

Meet Flashcards

Memory's best friend is repetition, repetition, repetition; yes, that stuff you hear about repeating things three times does actually work. To make review easier, make Flashcards for all the information that you need to study. All terms and vocabulary should be written on Flashcards and reviewed, both aloud and silently/mentally, before an exam. For students who have trouble writing or really messy handwriting, consider using one of the computer programs that allows you to type and print your Flashcards.

Steps to Creating Flashcards

Step 1: Write word to be memorized is written on the front side.

Step 2: Divide the backside into four quadrants.

Step 3: Write the definition or translation in the upper left quadrant.

Step 4: Draw a picture describing the word or fact in the upper right quadrant.

Step 5: Write a content story in the lower left quadrant.

Step 6: Create a sentence using the word in the lower right quadrant.

To aid with a better visualization, here is a template for what a good flashcard looks like.

Front

Chapter Number

Word/Fact

Back

Translation or definition (that actually makes sense to you)	Clue (picture, mneumonic device, or any hint that will help you remember the word)
Synonym	Sentence using the word (must show definition)

Studying from Flashcards

Step 1: Read the front and back of the card out loud three times.

Step 2: Test yourself by looking at the front of the card and repeating the information on the back without looking.

Step 3: Set aside cards that you cannot recall easily.

Step 4: Review cards that you are having difficulty with an additional two times.

Step 5: Quiz yourself on the entire set of cards.

Meet Voice Recorder

Sometimes hearing information repeated is a helpful tool. For this memory exercise you will need a Voice Recorder. The steps are similar to our flashcard method but instead of writing you will speak. Since electronics like dictation recorders (even digital ones) are probably not the most commonly found item in your household, try using software programs (like Garageband or Mixcraft) to record straight onto your computer. If you have any type of mp3 player, you can make sure that this study device travels with you for you to use whenever and wherever. Similarly, if you prefer having visual cues to help memorize, these programs also include VIDI features, so you can snag images from the Internet (or a CD copy of your textbook) to amp up your recording. If you don't have a portable mp3 player, you might consider using YouTube or a similar web sharing site to have access to a recording you've made anywhere you can get online.

Steps to Preparing the Recording

Step 1: After hitting the record button on the device of your choice, state the word/fact to be memorized, clearly and distinctly.

Step 2: Pause, then repeat the word/fact, followed by its definition (for a foreign language, say the definition in English).

Step 3: Pause, then repeat the word/fact, followed by another word clue or context.

Studying from the Recording

Step 1: Listen to the word.

Step 2: Say the definition.

Step 3: Listen to definition/context clue.

Step 4: Repeat word, definition, and context.

Meet Mind Maps

Another great tool is Mind Maps. Creating Mind Maps is powerful graphic technique which provides a way to sort information in a more visual way.

Steps to Creating a Mind Map

You will start with a concept or a main idea, and write it down in the middle of a blank page. From here, you'll add branches to related ideas, stemming away from the center, or central, idea. Keep the following concepts in mind.

» **Emphasis:** Use color, shape, and lettering to make important things stand out.

» **Association:** Connect ideas with arrows and branches.

» **Clarity:** Make sure your mind map is neat.

» **Hierarchy:** The main topic/general idea should be in the middle. As you branch out the concepts should be more concrete.

» **Relationships:** Look for connections between branches.

Let's take a look at an example for studying eukaryotic cells:

Mind Map—Eukaryotic Cells

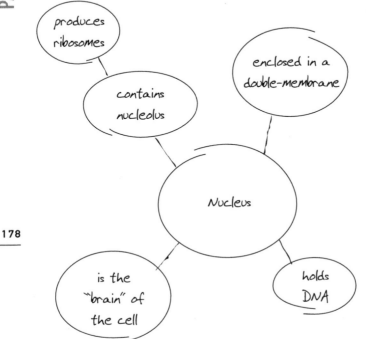

Studying from Mind Maps

Step 1: Read facts and explain the relationships between other facts.

Step 2: Leave parts of the mind map blank and fill it in based on the relationships.

Meet Outline

When you have a lot of material that you have to memorize, need to organize your notes, or gather information from reading, using the Outline method is very useful. Outlining is a way of streamlining and organizing all of the material you have to cover. It is especially helpful in creating a "to-go" study guide.

Steps to Creating an Outline

We introduced outlining when we talked about taking book notes (see page 108), and the same template can be used in your study process. In the course of studying, you may decide to re-read your notes or texts. You can simultaneously review your Outline and add in additional detailed points, or you may decide to take brand new notes and compare to your first try. Both are strong means of committing the information you're reviewing to mind. Here's a snapshot:

I. General Idea
    A. Evidence
        1. Supporting Detail and Explanation
        2. Supporting Detail and Explanation
    B. Evidence
        1. Supporting Detail and Explanation
        2. Supporting Detail and Explanation

C. Evidence

    1. Supporting Detail and Explanation

    2. Supporting Detail and Explanation

Studying from an Outline

Step 1: Turn the headings into questions and cover up the details to test yourself.

Step 2: Read the details and name the theme/topic to test yourself on the bigger idea.

Meet the Three-Fold Sheet

As we said, memory's best friend is repetition, and for some students, Flashcards are a great and easy method for review. However, if you don't like Flashcards or have a tendency to lose individual cards, consider using the Three-Fold Device. You can use this device for self-quizzing; it is also beneficial if you need to keep track of, compare, or memorize distinct information. By making a Three-Fold Sheet, you create a visual and written database of information. The Three-Fold Device is helpful for reviewing key terms for any class, and especially handy when studying vocabulary (for a foreign language or English).

Steps to Making the Three-Fold Sheet

Step 1: Grab a sheet of paper and fold it into three equal parts.

Step 2: In the first column, write the original term or word. In the second column, write the definition or the spelling of the word in the foreign language. Leave the third column to practice writing the spelling or definition.

Here's an example:

English	Francais	
cat	chat	
dog	chien	
fish	poisson	
turtle	tortue	
lizard	lézard	

Studying from Three-Fold Sheets

Step 1: Read the first two columns of the list out loud three times.

Step 2: Fold the paper so that you can see only of the one columns.

Step 3: Read the prompt and determine the information on the other side of the page.

Step 4: Star words/facts that you cannot recall easily.

Step 5: Review words that you are having difficulty with an additional two times.

Step 6: Quiz yourself on the entire list of terms, and write out your answer in the third column. Be sure to test yourself in all directions.

CHAPTER 10

Making Sense of the Stuff You've Studied

So far, you've studied your class notes, your textbook, your homework assignments, and any worksheets and additional notes you may have made. However, this is not enough to get you that grade you're striving for. Yes, we know, you've been studying hard, and you know the material inside and out, but having done this is not quite enough to achieve the grade you would expect to receive. You may not realize it, but you probably haven't synthesized the information into a more meaningful or applicable fashion. We're not discounting all of the work you've already invested in learning the material to be tested, but in order to really ensure that you will see the results you want, you should consider the studying you've done as solid groundwork to continue building on.

Perhaps you're a detail-oriented person, and you've studied each and every component of the topic to be tested. However, this does not necessarily mean you understand what each of these fine points means on a larger scale. Similarly, you might be someone who sees the forest more easily than the trees, and know each aspect of the concept you'll be evaluated on, but are still having a bit of difficulty with the particulars, and you have that, "Oh yeah, I know that" reaction after testing your knowledge of the small facts that comprise larger concept that you do understand.

Your teacher expects you to be able to zoom in and zoom out of the topic being tested, and show how the views relate to each other. We're going to show you how to approach this from forwards and from backwards (sort of like photosynthesis and cellular respiration ☺). You can pick the direction you typically find yourself going in. Here, alternate study methods are particularly helpful in getting your brain to put the finer points together with the bigger picture. For a more thorough approach to Study Devices, refer back to the previous chapter.

Zooming Out—Finding the Bigger Picture

If you happen to be one of those people who has a mind like a sponge and can absorb or retain every tiny minutiae of an event, or can recite every formula of a given chapter of a math textbook, you should focus on putting that photographic memory of yours to use in a larger context. In order to be able to zoom out, you should look for the larger, umbrella topics—you'll find these in your textbooks' headings and subheadings, in your class notes, or on your syllabus (if your teacher gives you one). Here's how to do it:

Step 1: Lay out all of your facts, depending on how you've studied them in the first place (whether you've chosen to make Flashcards, write out a list, or some combination of the two). Go through your notes and text to make sure that you haven't overlooked a given term.

Step 2: Determine what the main aspects of the topic of study are. Again, your texts and notes will help guide you in deciding what these are. Pay particular attention to various ways your teacher presents material; you'll likely find that certain terms are listed in your notes under larger topic headings, especially in your history, English and foreign language classes. For example, a memorable way to analyze a given historical period is in terms of S.P.E.R.M.: Social, Political, Economic, Religious, and Military viewpoints. (It might seem silly now, but it's certainly memorable, which is handy in test situations!)

Step 3: Organize your facts into the various main idea categories. Here, your initial mode of studying does come into play. Depending on whether you prefer lists vs. charts vs. Flashcards vs. Outline vs. your-choice, you should again pick the method that works best for you to organize the fine details of a topic into bigger categories. Your goal here is to connect each detail, formula, or fact that you've studied to the main topic or idea, specifically in terms of how it relates to the topic. If you've made Flashcards, you can practice this by grouping the cards into various topic piles, and going through each to determine how the card's fact relates to the topic. If you're more of a list or chart person, you can create another sheet with the facts arranged together according to the topic they relate to; be sure to include a column or space where you can jot down the how of the relationship between the two.

We've included a couple of worksheets for you to use as a template to organize those details you know into relevant conceptual groupings. The worksheet on the facing page will help you get started from a Zooming Out point of view.

Zooming In—Picking Out the "Lil Things"

Not everyone is lucky enough to have a photographic memory. If you can recall only various bits and pieces, but have a very strong grasp of what the core facets of a given topic are, then it's best to work from a top-down perspective to solidify shakier ground. For example, if you can thoroughly discuss the plot of an entire novel

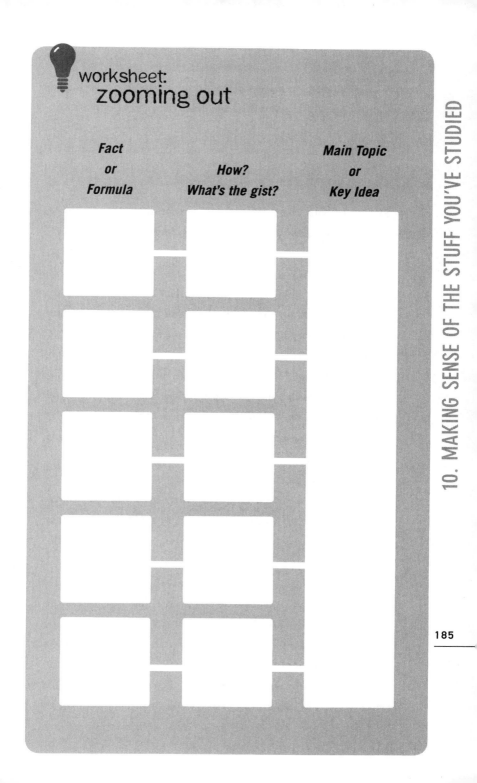

worksheet:
zooming out

Fact or Formula

How? What's the gist?

Main Topic or Key Idea

and its multiple themes, but do not have a clue as to what the characters' names are nor do you know who wrote the thing, you need to work from your big picture view down to the nitty gritty. Again, depending on your preferred method of studying, the way in which you go about connecting your forest to those troublesome trees might differ somewhat, but here are some ideas for where to start.

Step 1: Lay out your foundation. This means, since you have a good understanding of the topic and its various aspects, work from your strengths down to the stuff that you fumble. Often, it's most helpful to consult your class notes and textbooks to get an accurate view of wording, terms, and diverse elements to analyze the main topic of study. Again, look to the chapter headings and sub-headings for the biggest clues about how to break down the main subject. These topic headings are observing what the big picture is from the top of a top-down view.

Step 2: Figure out what the bigger puzzle is made of—what are the pieces? You know where you're starting from; now it's time to figure out what makes up the larger concepts. If you've made note cards to remember specifics, group them together under a larger idea that you've derived in Step 1 (from notes, text, chapter headings, etc.). Similarly, if you wrote up a list of key terms or facts, organize them into groups that hit the components of the topic that you're familiar with in a separate list or chart.

For example, if you are studying the behavior of gases in chemistry, you probably know how ideal gases behave under given conditions (they collide with total elasticity, one mole will occupy 22.4L at STP, etc.). You also may recall a memorable Acronym for memorizing the chemical elements that exist as diatomic molecules: H.O.N.Cl.Br.I.F. (Note: there are a couple permutations of this, like Br.I.N.Cl.H.O.F. or H.O.F.Br.I.N.Cl.; choose the one that you remember best). Knowing the behavior of gases (the gist of the topic) and additionally knowing the seven diatomics Acronym, you should be able to tackle a problem in which you are asked to determine what happens to a given amount of nitrogen gas under given circumstances. Basically, your firm understanding of the top can help you work out the down pieces, if you focus on how the two are related.

Step 3: Practice juggling the pieces. Each fact does not necessarily belong solely under one heading or category; a given detail can be used to demonstrate key aspects of the larger topic being tested. Try mixing the details into the different category headings you know are crucial to the main topic, and test yourself by tying a given factoid to several categories.

Let's say you're studying *Romeo and Juliet* in your English class. You can recite the plot with good accuracy and the running themes of destiny vs. free will, innocence, pride; you also know that there are two sides of characters but you keep forgetting their names and allegiances. However, your teacher assigns you a short essay in which you are given a quote, and asked to identify the speaker, context, and meaning. Don't freak out if you don't immediately understand the quote, let alone recognize it at all.

Here's a prime example of when to use your top strengths. Start by running through the themes you know for certain run throughout the play. You've likely studied the main characters, plot points, and key terms as they relate to the main themes, so you're likely to recognize at least one of these components in the quote. This recognition of a character, plot point, or vocabulary term should trigger a connection you studied between this trigger and either a given character or context. From here, you're likely to formulate an accurate response to the assignment without getting too caught up in detail-mongering. You'll find a sample worksheet that can help you organize your down pieces to make up your top on the following page.

worksheet:
zooming in

**Main Topic
or
Key Idea**

**How?
What's the gist?**

**Fact
or
Formula**

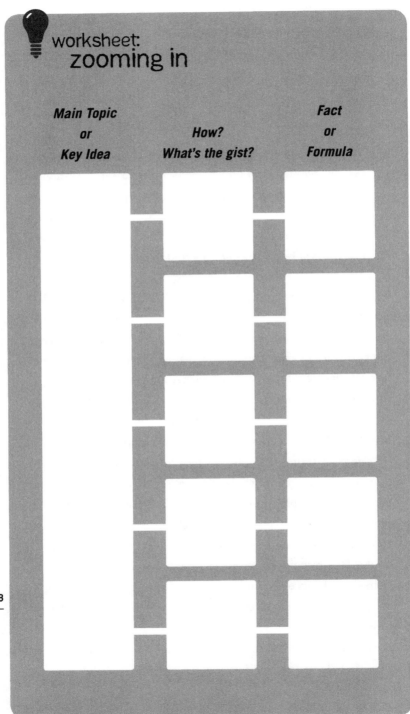

Taming the Test Monster: What the Formats Are, and Why You Should Care

Finally, we've gotten to the part where we confront the beast: your upcoming test! In this chapter, we'll examine the monster from the angles of what you'll be seeing, what you might be thinking or feeling while doing the thing, and how you can improve how to tackle a test based on what your graded results are.

Tests come in many different shapes, colors and sizes. In order to be able to recognize each format (which is which), we're going to take you through a mock example of each. By doing this, we can show you what your teacher wants to know and why she is asking this of you. There are specific ways to prepare for each type of test, so it's important to know what kind of questions you'll be asked so that you can study in the most effective way for it. It's sort of like playing tennis with a tennis racket instead of a baseball bat—both Devices are capable of hitting the ball, but one makes more sense to use given the circumstance(s). It's the same as wearing tennis shoes on a soccer field instead of cleats where one would clearly be more appropriate and effective.

True/False Questions

A true-false (T/F) test is the most straightforward type of explicit memory test, and is typically presented in one of two formats. In the first, you pick whether a statement is true or false. In the second, in addition to evaluating whether or not a statement is true or false, you must be able to correct any possible false statements. These T/F questions are designed to test your knowledge of a given subject or section. That is, your teacher wants to know if you know your stuff.

Here's an example question, in which you'd answer true (T) or false (F):

Mitochondria is/are the control center of a eukaryotic cell.

The gist of the T/F questions is that you either know the answer to a question (which, if you're curious here, is false), or you don't. Preparation for T/F questions is pretty much just straight memorization of facts. These questions don't really get at a deep level of analysis or connection of concepts or underlying themes; you are just being tested on your ability to regurgitate what you know. Often teachers will give T/F questions about facts such as: dates (history), names/important figures, document titles or events (history, science, English). Sometimes you'll get the oddball/screwball question about some obscure factoid that your teacher mentioned in class as being important—this pretty much is aimed at seeing whether or not you paid enough attention in class to write this point down.

Because T/F questions are aimed at specific pieces of knowledge that you've memorized, you have to use the strategies that work for you to allow you to remember facts and details. As discussed in the previous section, anything from Flashcards to charts, lists, and mnemonic devices are good ways to get these facts into your head. A great way to practice for T/F questions is to create a Jeopardy-style game for yourself, where you can clump together specific facts in a way that can help you organize and chunk together facts in an easier-to-memorize manner. This is also a fun way to study for these tests with your friends.

Fill-in-the-Blank, Matching, and Definitions Questions

Fill-in the blank, matching, and definitions questions are similar to T/F questions in many ways. These questions test exact facts and do not require you to connect the facts to greater themes. Preparation for these types of questions should include rote memorization using Flashcards, lists, and mneumonic devices. It could also be helpful to create quizzes to test your memory. When preparing for these types of tests remember that there is often more than one way to define a word, so your preparation should include exploration of the most common definitions of words and not just the shortest one!

Standardized and Multiple Choice Questions

Standardized or multiple choice tests can be similar to T/F questions, in that they test whether you know a given fact based on a small amount of information given to you (the lead-in/overhang), but they can also be targeting something a bit more complex. Here, your teacher can ask you to evaluate which answer is more correct for the question asked (you usually end up choosing between two answers). Your ability to see a common thread/theme between the choices given (all of the above/none of the above), or even both of these at the same time is what is being tested.

A good way to study for this type of question is to organize your facts. For example, if you have written out facts on note cards, you can quiz yourself on how one card relates to another. You can create separate piles for cards that deal with a specific over-arching idea that was discussed in class. By learning one pile at a time, you create mental associations between these facts. Also, try switching up the piles and see how many topic piles you can create. Another game-like study method is to spread out a given number of note cards in a five by five square, and pick any two of these cards and state how they relate to each other. In pairing up your facts, you put the information more firmly in your mind than you would by simply memorizing each individual fact separately.

Here's an example question:

Which of the following characters is murdered in Shakespeare's Romeo and Juliet?
1. *The Prince*
2. *Paris*
3. *Lady Capulet*
4. *Tybalt*
5. *All of the above*

Short Answer Questions

Short answer questions are really just factually based questions, like multiple choice questions, in disguise. These questions are typically intimidating just because of the massive amount of white page space on which they appear, which makes you think you have to write more than is necessary. Your teacher will usually ask short answer questions to see if you know what a given term means and why it is important. In studying for these types of questions, your main focus should be the facts themselves and how they relate to a bigger concept. When studying for these types of questions, you should ask yourself and be able to answer the following two questions: What is it, and why do I care?

Here are a couple of example questions:

Identify the following important historical figure: Otto von Bismarck

Explain Henry Hudson's fur trade and its importance in pre-Colonial America.

Essay Questions

Unlike the above three types of questions, essays are a completely different type of question. Just knowing your facts is only going to get you started. You have to be able to use these facts to demonstrate a larger idea. When teachers ask essay questions, they're interested in seeing that you not only know the facts, but how to connect these things to one another. Oftentimes when teachers create and grade essays, they do so with a rubric—this is basically a list of key points you should include in your essay, such as specific factual information, and links between these details that support a solid thesis/theme interpretation. The test also checks your ability to write in proper, grammatically correct English. In studying for an essay, it's important to keep your focus on the main question being asked, then take that main concept and explain the how and why of it.

Now It's Your Turn: Practicing for the Test

So, you've made it through all of your studying, right?? You're most certainly thinking something like, "What else could there possibly be that I have to do??" There's one last piece to cover to make sure you'll get the most out of all the work you've done so far. Yes, we know you really have done a lot already: you took all of your Daily Maintenance Work and created Study Devices, which you then pieced together into bigger perspectives (and depending on which direction, Zooming In or Zooming Out, you found you needed to bulk up more). Well, you've now put yourself in a prime position to strike at the test, so practice doing exactly that! Quizzing yourself on all levels of depth of understanding is the final step to sealing the deal of a good grade. Here, we'll talk about two ways of doing exactly that: Mock Tests and alternative quizzing methods.

Mock Tests

Before you head into taking the real test, putting yourself through a mock test is a great way to figure out exactly how ready you are. Grab your textbook, homework assignments, notes, quizzes or interim tests, your Study Devices and Daily Maintenance Work, and organize these materials in an order that makes the most sense for you. We typically recommend going chronologically, in the order in which your teacher presented the material, start to finish. However, if you prefer to really push yourself, organize your materials from the most to least difficult challenging material for you (or vice versa, if you'd rather ease your way in).

Set up your mock test based on the format of old tests you've taken, so that what you're practicing resembles what you're going to be doing in class. We'll go into more detail about test formats in the next chapter. For sample questions, you have plenty at your disposal, found in all of the study materials you've gathered and organized. In going through your study resources, focus on problems or questions that took you longer to resolve or figure out. For example, pick homework questions that either took you a longer time to solve or you answered incorrectly the first time. Similarly, if you find areas in your notes that you highlighted or circled with the so you could revisit them or meet with your teacher to review, formulate questions regarding these iffy topics. Putting together your own test is an extremely effective study tool in itself, since you're not just testing the information, but also juggling several ways in which the material can be tested.

If your class uses a textbook, you will often find that there is a chapter review section, which covers topics from each portion of the given chapter. This can be used as a mock test itself, but hopefully you won't stop at doing just this one! This section will include questions ranging from concept review to computation or application questions, presented in various formats that you can choose from to suit your teacher's test requirements (multiple choice, T/F, short answer, etc.). However, if you've already covered these questions as homework or otherwise, you can also look to see if there is a textbook-related website that will offer more questions that cover the same material.

In addition to these, if you are studying for a unit test that covers more than one chapter, it's likely that you've already had at least one quiz on part of the material already. You can use the questions from the quiz or quizzes (particularly those you didn't quite get) as a template or as actual questions on your mock test. The best resource to create your Mock Tests from is your Daily Maintenance Workbook (which is why you should keep one ☺). Here, you've compiled an arsenal of questions that cover material that you don't have a firm grasp on yet, but will once you've included and redone these problems in a mock test.

If there will be essays included on your test, make sure you review your class notes for any additional hints from your teacher. These essay questions are not picked at random, but are chosen as specific areas of focus that your teacher will have at the least mentioned, if not stressed/emphasized, as important ideas/concepts during class. Hopefully, you will have made a note of this in your class notes, and perhaps even translated this into your Daily Maintenance Work. The length of your mock test will ideally reflect the real test you'll take, but you might prefer to break up your testing into smaller portions.

Once you've created a mock test, it's important to set yourself up in an environment that is like one in the real test's setting. That is, try and pick a place that you will feel like it's a bit more of a formal setting than just sitting in your bedroom. Also part of this environment is the noise level. Your teachers don't tolerate talking during tests, so consider going to a library or quiet diner near your house instead of the local Starbucks, bookstore, or staying home where you can potentially be distracted by your siblings, parents, friends online, etc.

After creating a mock test and taking it in a timed fashion (use an egg/oven timer or stopwatch if you have one handy, but if not, a wristwatch or wall clock will do just fine), go over it in the way that your teacher would. Grade yourself in red (or your teacher's typical color of choice), and if you find yourself correcting or add-ing notes in color onto your timed work, using your study materi-als as the answer key, stop and mark down what concepts you're finding fault with—these are the areas you're not quite fluent with and should focus on more in your studies. If you feel like you still need more practice, have a friend make up a test of her own with a different set of questions. Make a copy of the mock test you cre-ated, and then swap yours with your friend's.

If you still feel like you're not quite sure how to go about mak-ing up your own mock test, you can use the basic template on the facing page to get started.

Mixing It Up:
Alternative Means of Quizzing Yourself

You've done a pretty thorough rundown on the subject of study-ing, so let's try something a bit different. The alternative testing methods we'll go through here will further strengthen your grasp of the material and train your brain to be able to not just spit back the facts, but also to be able to make connections and use the infor-mation that you've studied in a more complex fashion. This means that your brain will be more like the athlete who is able to compete successfully in any sport, versus the one who only specializes in a specific area. How can you get to be this versatile mastermind? Practice, of course, but now we'll suggest a few tactics that differ from your average drill.

We will only give a few examples of the types of games you can create for yourself so that you can stay engaged in your study-ing without getting bored, zoning out, or just going through the motions. Hopefully, these gaming ideas will spark others that you come up with yourself. We know it's tough to constantly trudge through learning material from start to finish, and we find that

worksheet:
mock test generator

Title(s)/Chapter(s) of Topic Covered:

Write appropriate Terms/Formulas/Definitions in this box.

Write examples in this box.

Write Sample Problems in this box.

playing games like the ones we describe help keep your mind focused on the material. Even better, you can actually get your friends involved, and clarify any misunderstandings you might not have caught on your own. Plus, it's always more fun to play with a friend. **Note:** the games we describe here are easy to apply to any subject, and are much easier to start if you've already made out study Flashcards.

Jeopardy

Jeopardy can be played with two participants but it is preferable to have at least three. There is no limit to how many players take part in the game.

Here's what you'll need:

» At least one other person to play against (preferably a classmate, who also might benefit from the studying)

» Someone to be the host (and fact-checker)

» Flashcards

» Notes/textbook

» Buzzer (a pot, drum, or anything that produces a loud noise will work well)

» Pen and paper to keep score

Here's what to do:

1. Begin by creating categories pertinent to the subject you're studying. For example, for Algebra 1, good headings are: "Exponent Rules," "Linear Equations," and "Polynomials."

2. Under each category, make at least five question cards. The front of each card should have a point value. Label the back of the card with a keyword, answer to a specific question, or a short question.

3. If there is more than one player, to start the game the "host" will pick a number between one and twenty and the person who guesses closest will take the first turn; the player that guesses second closest will take the second turn, etc.

4. On each turn, the player will select a specific card from the category and the host will turn over the card and read the question.

5. After the question is read by the host, the players buzz (or bang) to have the opportunity to answer the question. The player who buzzes first will take the first attempt at responding.

6. If the question is answered correctly then the player receives the allotted points on the card. However, if the question is answered incorrectly, then the points are decreased from the responder's score and the other players can take a shot at answering the question (again, by buzzing). Once the question is answered correctly, the card should be removed from the board.

7. Players should keep track of questions that they answer incorrectly or categories that they feel rusty on so that these topics can be reviewed after the game.

8. It is the responsibility of the host to confirm the correct response. Keep notes and textbooks handy for reference.

When all the cards have been eliminated from the board, the points can be calculated. The player with the most points wins!

Categories

This game can be played with just one person, but to add a competitive element, additional players can participate. Categories is excellent for any fact-based content, such as for English and history.

Here's what you'll need:

- » A timer
- » Flashcards
- » Notes/textbook
- » Pen and paper (for each player)

Here's what to do:

1. Start by labeling Flashcards with broad categories that are pertinent to the subject you're studying. Each card should have one category. For example, for a literature exam, good categories are: "Protagonists," "Main Themes," and "Recurring Symbols."

2. Label each sheet of paper from one to ten.

3. Set the timer for two minutes and grab the first category card.

4. On your sheet of paper, list as many responses as possible that fit into the category card.

5. When time is up, calculate how many connections you were able to list for the category and add one point per correct response to your score.

6. For bonus points, give one correct explanation as to how the responses are connected to the category.

7. Keep going until you've gone through all of the Flashcards you've made, and whoever has the most points tallied at the end, wins!

Go Fish

For this game you're challenged to connect ideas and facts. You can play either as a single player or as an entire class, by taking turns.

Here's what you'll need:

» Flashcards
» Notes/textbook

Here's what to do:

1. Start by creating two piles of Flashcards: one for facts and another for broader concepts. Foreign languages can be practiced by putting vocabulary or verbs in the fact pile, and concept pile, containing types of conjugations, subjects of sentences, or tenses.

2. Once you've created and separated these two piles of cards, shuffle and place them in front of you. Draw one card from the top of each pile. Connect the two concepts. For example, if you picked a card with the Spanish verb "bailar" from the fact pile, and a card saying "Use in a present tense sentence," employ the appropriate present tense conjugation to a subject of your choice. If a verb (like "bailar") is drawn, and the concept card reads "perro," construct a sentence (in a tense of your choosing).

3. Continue playing through until you've completed the fact and concept pile, making sure to have addressed all cards in both piles. You can easily reshuffle and recycle cards (especially for the concept pile) if necessary, having finished off one pile but not the other.

Spitfire

This game is more a test of your accuracy under fire. This is particularly useful in math, geography, and chemistry. Also, this is a great way to help improve your Time Management for test situations.

Here's what you need:

- » Someone who can be a game master (a friend, parent, sibling, or even yourself will suffice)
- » For a competitive edge, play with friends
- » Master list of questions
- » Two blank sheets of paper and a pen/pencil (per player)
- » Timer (stopwatch, oven timer, wall clock, etc. are fine)
- » Notes/textbook
- » NO calculators or other materials allowed!

Here's what to do:

1. Write up a master list of ten questions for round one. For each subsequent round, you can add one to two questions.

2. Give the list to the game master. If you are filling this role, set the questions where they are easy to view. Make sure to have your paper, writing utensil, and timer ready.

3. Set your timer for two minutes (or note the time and set an alarm), and start timing yourself when you begin to answer the first question. Work your way through all of the problems as best you can within the time constraints, and put your pen/pencil down when time's up.

4. Check your answers and give yourself one point for every correct answer and subtract one point for every incorrect answer.

5. For the following rounds you can repeat steps one through four, but add one to two questions to each master list so that you can challenge yourself to increase the speed at which you answer questions.

Bingo

This approach tests your ability to recall under fire, as you'll likely be playing against another player. Similarly, this Device tests your grasp of rote facts. To start a new game, simply pick up the Post-its and rearrange the playing grid.

Here's what you need:

» Pad of Post-it squares (three by three or smaller)
» Pens/pencils
» Set of nine or sixteen index cards
» Notes/textbook
» One piece of paper per player (or you could simply use a flat surface, such as cookie sheet or the kitchen table)
» A set of bingo chips, about ten per player (such as plastic chips, bottle caps, paper clips, coins, macaroni, MandMs)

Here's what to do:

1. Write thirty specific questions, math problems, or vocabulary on the index cards. Use one question per card.
2. Put the stack of index cards face down.
3. Write the answers to the questions on the Post-its.
4. Arrange the notes in a square on the construction paper or flat surface. If you're playing with nine answers, arrange them in three rows of three. For sixteen answers, four rows of four. You will have left over Post-its that can be used for future games.
5. The first player turns over the top index card and reads the question aloud.
6. Players mark the answer to the question on the Post-it note with a bingo marker.
7. Once everyone's done marking, put the card in the discard pile.
8. Continue in this manner until a player has' marked an entire row on their bingo board. The winner yells, "Bingo!"

Trivial Pursuit

This game is particularly useful in targeting specifics of a subject, such as in a science, history, or English class. The game aims to improve your accuracy and recall under fire for test situations, as well as getting your brain to consider possible and more complex connections between various concepts; it's particularly helpful in preparing for essays.

Here's what you need:

» Cards of facts
» Reference table or cards of categories to be tested
» Color-coded playing pieces (these should correspond to the category colors chosen)
» Game board (it helps if it's already an actual Trivial Pursuit board, but you can color code any game board to suit your needs)
» Set of dice
» Score card paper and pen
» Textbook/notes (for post-answer reference only)
» For a more competitive edge, play with friends

Here's what to do:

1. Create a set of note cards containing all of the relevant facts for a given topic, in as detailed a fashion as possible. Also, create five to eight separate category headings and color code them on note cards or in different pen or marker on a separate sheet, such as a time period/era (e.g., 1215-1789 A.D., the Enlightenment, etc.), important figures (examples of these include main characters in a novel, primary components of a cell, and historical leaders or philosophers/thinkers). For more complex and higher levels of challenge, you should designate such categories as S.P.E.R.M., for example

(to review: S=Social, P=Political, E=Economic, R=Religious, and M=Military).

2. If you're playing with others, roll the die to see the order in which you will play (highest rolled number goes first, second highest second, etc.). If it's just you, pick a category (color) through which you'll work, and set the appropriate playing piece in the designated starting space.

3. For each turn, roll the die, and according to which color you land on, you will be asked to relate the fact drawn from the card pile to the corresponding category. For every accurate answer given, award yourself a point. If you are unable to answer within a three-minute time period, your turn expires, and the next player rolls.

4. Check your answers against your notes or text, and give yourself one point for every correct answer. It's most helpful if you have a game master to rule whether an answer is valid or not, but it isn't necessary.

Repeat steps one through four. The first player to answer one question in each category correctly wins.

A Subject-Based Way to Apply Study Devices

So, now that we've gone through how to study for a test, let's apply all of the approaches to each subject. You've planned when to study and what to study for each subject, you know which approaches work for you, and you know what to expect on each test. We will discuss subject-specific study steps for all the classes that you will encounter and show you how to apply the Study Devices when appropriate. Again, it's important to consider which means of studying you find most effective when choosing which Study Devices to use for which subject.

Math

If you have completed all your homework and kept up with Daily Maintenance Work, then you can skip this section. However, since nobody is perfect and sometimes our best intentions don't work out properly, let's talk about what you should do if you didn't quite keep up with either your homework or Daily Maintenance Work.

Since math is learned by doing problems, take all your old homework assignments and Worksheet: Mock Test Generator. Re-write all the problems that you answered incorrectly the first time around. Solve the problems for practice. Check your answers by comparing them to the homework or asking a class buddy for the correct answers. If you are still having trouble, write out the problems and talk to your teacher before or after class.

In addition to practice problems, you will probably have to memorize formulas and some concepts. You should write out all the formulas that you will need to memorize on Worksheet: Mock Test Generator. One of the best ways to actually memorize the information is by making Flashcards. Use these transportable study aids to memorize formulas. If you are having trouble memorizing something or a particular concept is just not sinking in, get help before it is too late. Ask your teacher to go over the glitch you might be having.

By studying your Flashcards and doing Daily Maintenance Work, or the more last-minute form of Maintenance Work, you are guaranteeing a thorough understanding of concepts. The next step is transferring the conceptual knowledge to test know-how. The best way to be prepared for a test is by creating Mock Tests. Grab your textbook, homework assignments, and the study sheet you have from you Daily Maintenance Work. Take the last piece of Worksheet: Mock Test Generator and create a practice test. Have a friend do the same thing, but with a different set of questions. Make a copy of the mock test you created and switch with a friend.

Steps for Studying for Math-Based Tests

Step 1: Do problems from old homework assignments.

Step 2: Make Flashcards with terms and formulas.

Step 3: Create Mock Tests from Daily Maintenance Work.

The review sheet below can be used to format the study process. It is most helpful if stapled together and inserted into your binder.

Sciences: Biology, Chemistry, and Physics

If you have completed all your homework and kept-up with Daily Maintenance Work, then you can skip this section. However, since nobody is perfect and sometimes our best intentions don't work out properly, let's talk about what you should do if you didn't quite keep up with either your homework or Daily Maintenance Work. Since science is learned by doing problems, take all your old homework assignments and Worksheet: Mock Test Generator. Rewrite all the problems that you answered incorrectly the first time around. Solve the problems for practice. Check your answers by comparing them to the homework or asking a class buddy for the correct answers. If you are still having trouble, write out the problems and talk to your teacher before or after class.

In addition to practice problems, you will probably have to memorize formulas and some concepts. You should write out all the formulas that you will need to memorize on Worksheet: Mock Test Generator. One of the best ways to actually memorize the information is by making Flashcards. Use these transportable study aids to memorize formulas. If you are having trouble memorizing something or a particular concept is just not sinking in, get help before it is too late. Ask your teacher to go over the glitch you might be having.

By studying your Flashcards and doing Daily Maintenance Work, or the more last-minute form of Maintenance Work, you are guaranteeing a thorough understanding of concepts. The next step is transferring the conceptual knowledge to test know-how. The best way to be prepared for a test is by creating Mock Tests. Grab your textbook, homework assignments, and the study sheet you have from you Daily Maintenance Work. Take the last piece of Worksheet: Mock Test Generator and create a practice test. Have a friend do the same thing but with a different set of questions. Make a copy of the mock test you created and switch with a friend.

Studying for Science Tests
Step 1: Do problems from old homework assignments.
Step 2: Make Flashcards with terms and formulas.
Step 3: Create Mock Tests from Daily Maintenance Work.

History

Humanities subjects will be approached differently than math- or science-based subjects. Your job in preparing for these types of subjects will be to fully understand concepts and be capable of applying your knowledge in short answer, essay, and multiple choice questions. Therefore, you will concentrate less on doing practice problems and more on conceptual understanding.

The first step to studying should be looking at your test Outline, finding the topics that will be covered on the tests, and reviewing by re-reading the textbook and class notes and creating an Outline. The process of preparing an Outline will help you make sense of information and memorize facts. While you are creating Outlines you may also want to make Flashcards. Although it may seem redundant, the process of writing the important information twice will do wonders for your memory and the Flashcards are a more portable tool than Outlines.

When you feel comfortable with the information, use your Flashcards and Outlines to self-test. Quiz yourself with your

Flashcards or by covering up parts of the Outline and filling in the blanks. You can also make a copy of the Outlines and white-out terms, facts, dates, etc. and fill them in from memory. Grab the important event sheet and quiz yourself with it. Practicing writing longer responses is also important. Through the Daily Maintenance Work, test outlining, and review process you have probably zeroed in on important topics. Identify a few themes or concepts and write longer responses. If possible, have your teacher, parent, or friend read over your essay.

For more details on how best to create a mock test, refer back to Taming the Test Monster on page 189.

Studying for Memory-Based Subjects

Step 1: Create Outline from notes and textbook.

Step 2: Make Flashcards of terms.

Step 3: Quiz yourself using Flashcards.

Step 4: Practice multiple-choice questions.

English

English tests come in all different shapes and sizes, but most of them require understanding facts and memorization. Whether you're being tested on vocabulary words, grammar, names of characters, or the name of Shakespeare's theater, you'll want to begin by using a study device that will help you get the facts in your head. Using Flashcards or word lists is a great way to make the information stick. Remember to quiz yourself with your Flashcards or by covering up parts of lists. You can practice using vocabulary in sentences, and try to place your characters in specific scenes in order to get a well-rounded understanding of the material.

Your English class will probably have a focus on literature. Beyond just reading stories, your teacher wants you to have an understanding of themes and important trends in a novel, short story, or poem and be able to think analytically and critically about these themes. It is important to understand and be able to explain why a character acts the way he does, and why this is important to the story as a whole. This type of understanding is often tested in short answer or short essay format. In preparing for these types of exams, you should begin by focusing your energy on reviewing bigger concepts that were covered. Creating Flashcards or a list that includes summaries, overarching themes, and common symbols will prepare you for most English tests.

The final step in preparing for an English test will be connecting the dots between factual information and thematic information. You will be asked to move back and forth between key themes, characters, scenes, and perhaps key terms. You will be asked to explain and draw conclusions as to how the smaller details, such as scenes and characters, support an overarching theme. The best way to prepare is to make a detailed Outline, including quotes, and show how different things support big-picture ideas and make the story what it is and why it is an important story to tell. You can also want to use your Flashcards by selecting two cards and connecting them based on your knowledge and understanding of the themes.

Studying for English Tests

Step 1: Make Flashcards for vocab or any fact-based information.

Step 2: Make a list or Outline of literary summaries, themes, and important points.

Step 3: Connect fact-based information from Step 1 and theme-based information from Step 2.

Step 4: Create Mock Tests from Daily Maintenance Work.

Foreign Language

When a student first begins foreign language studies, the focus of the class is primarily directed at cultivating two fundamental components: vocabulary and grammar. Any language is made up of words that are arranged in a specific order. In the study of a language, you need to memorize at least some of its words in order to be able to express yourself in cohesive, coherent sentences. What also matters all the more is your spelling—in foreign languages, there are specific notations (such as accents or tildes), that are crucial to being able to recognize the word and pronounce it properly.

One of the first things a teacher will tell you is that you need to have an unabridged English translation dictionary for the language you're studying. Make sure you get one. This tool will become your biggest asset as you move forward in your acquisition of the language. Don't trust translation websites or travel-companion sized dictionaries, as their versions of phrases are often oversimplified and way off target from what you had intended to say. Since each student learns differently, there are two main methods we recommend in approaching the memorization of such an enormous amount of individual pieces of information: Flashcards or lists.

The key to retaining what you memorize can be summed up in three words: practice, practice, practice!!! (Yeah, we know it's really one word emphasized three times). Sure, you've very likely heard this before, but your parents and teachers didn't make up the saying "practice makes perfect" just so they would have another pointless phrase to annoy you with.

Flashcards and lists are appropriate Tools for students who are working to increase their arsenal of words. These cards or lists should be reviewed regularly (daily). Your Flashcards or lists are your language currency. You can't get by without them, and in order for the cards to have value, they must be constantly used. Just because you make a set of cards or created a list for one particular night of work doesn't mean you've finished with them. At the end of a week, go through all of your vocabulary and test your retention, again setting aside those words you're unsure of for further review.

For both types of vocabulary review, practicing going from the foreign term to the English definition is not enough. You should also do the reverse, giving yourself the English definition and generating the right word. All review should include reading cards and lists out loud. The reason we place such importance on reading aloud is because this doubles the means of learning this language. You've not only read it, but you're becoming accustomed to hearing it. There are often sections of your tests that require that you listen to a tape recording and transcribe what was said. This is a backwards testing of your comprehension of your vocabulary.

The last, but not least valuable practice application is creating practice tests. In studying for tests, it's helpful to use any interim chapter quizzes, old tests, and homework assignments. Using Worksheet: Mock Test Generator you should create a practice test based on the format of previous exams. Use homework and quizzes for examples for practice problems. Once you've created a practice test you should close your books and take the exam under simulated conditions.

Studying Foreign Language

Step 1: Create vocabulary lists of new words.

Step 2: Make Flashcards from vocabulary lists.

Step 3: Maintain separate list of conjugation and grammar rules.

Step 4: Read study materials out loud.

Step 5: Create practice tests.

jake and bianca

Having helped each other make it through most of the academic year together, Jake and Bianca decide that it would be very helpful to study together for finals. At Bianca's urging, they spend part of a Saturday and Sunday four weeks before exams setting up a study schedule and gathering the necessary materials, including planners, textbooks, notes, and Maintenance Work.

Upon arriving at Bianca's after soccer practice later that week, and looking over all the materials they've now organized into piles that cover the huge dining table, Jake feels a creeping sense of being overwhelmed. Although he did plan what and when to study, he finds himself at a complete loss as to how to actually start. He plucks at a sheet from the top of one of the piles and tries reading over the randomly chosen notes, but the information just doesn't seem to stick. He glances over at Bianca who is looking over her meticulously ordered Flashcards and conjugation charts for Spanish. Taking her lead, he decides that he too will start with Spanish.

As he is constantly losing Flashcards, he decides that it's safer to make lists of words on a sheet of paper. Jake grabs some loose-leaf pages and his textbook, and beginning with the first chapter of the year, writes out each word in Spanish on the left side and the definition on the right. He works his way through all of the terms he gathers from the textbook chapters covered, class notes and homework. Then he staples the pages together and folds each of the sheets in half. Keeping the pages unfolded, he reads each word aloud and says the definition in English three times, much to Bianca's amusement and annoyance. Jake then folds the sheets in half and mentally quizzes himself, silently reading the definition then giving the Spanish term in his head. After some practice, Jake feels confident enough to suggest to Bianca that they quiz each other.

"First, how 'bout I give you the English word or definition, and you say the word in Spanish, and then we'll switch," Jake suggests.

"Ok," Bianca agrees, adding, "then we'll switch again and test each other by asking with the Spanish word and answering with the English definition."

The pair takes their turns quizzing each other, Bianca making fewer mistakes than Jake, until both are satisfied with what they know. Jake marks the words on his sheets that gave him more difficulty, and sits back, closing his eyes and hoping to relax. However, Bianca is already frowning at her vocab Flashcards.

"What about writing it out?"

Jake straightens, slowly opening his eyes. "Writing what out?"

"The vocab words!" Bianca exclaims. "We do need to know how to spell this stuff, where to put accents, tildes, when to use double l's instead of y's. . . ."

"Okay, okay, point taken," Jake interrupts tiredly. "Let's go through it one more time with asking definitions and spelling each answer, accents and all."

Bianca pauses, sensing how their quizzing has drained them somewhat of their initial energy, and decides that use of a new tactic is in order. "Well, that's getting kinda old. Let's get my mom to quiz us . . . Jeopardy-style!"

Jake hesitates while Bianca springs up to gather her cards, asking uncertainly, "Ok, but what's the winner gonna get?"

Bianca halts mid-reach. "Hmm. I don't know."

Jake leans back, eyeing B's videogame collection, and proposes slowly, "Well . . . if I win, then we get to play Wii for fifteen minutes."

Bianca grins. "Fine. And if I win, then we'll do whatever I want for fifteen minutes."

Jake shoots to his feet, self-consciously pulling at his shirt sleeves. "Hey, that's not fair. I want to know what I'm getting myself into. What do you want if you win?"

Bianca floats out the door, heading for the kitchen where her mom is on the phone, and gloatingly teases, "Hah. You'll just have to wait and see."

Bianca's mom willingly and enthusiastically plays the role of Alex Trebek, much to the pair's amusement. At the end of the game, Bianca and Jake realize that they forgot to keep score. Bianca decides to call it even, but Jake vehemently disagrees. "I totally won."

Bianca rolls her eyes at him, heading back to her room. "You always think you've won."

Jake follows and scoffs, "So, basically you agree with me. I've been thinking . . . ." Jake begins carefully. "Since I'm the champion and you owe me, you should go to the school dance with me. . . ."

"Oh, do you? What happened to the fifteen minute Wii break?" Bianca asks smugly, crossing her arms and observing Jake's obvious discomfort.

"Yeah . . . well, you know, just as friends. Hey, I won, so I get to pick my prize!" Jake protests defensively.

Bianca laughs, "Ok, just as friends, since you're such the Spanish Spelling Champ and all. So, I'll see you tomorrow for math and science review?"

Jake grins, and offers while packing his books, "Sure, how about my house next time?"

Bianca nods graciously, agreeing, "Sounds good. But don't forget to keep studying Spanish. I might just challenge you to round two tomorrow. We'll see who the real champion is then."

Jake adamantly brags, "No chance you're ever unseating me. I totally rocked that Spanish review."

Bianca smiles knowingly. "We shall see."

The next day, Bianca and Jake settle themselves at Jake's dining room table to review for their math and science finals. Applying their previous study procedure to science review, they both soon acknowledge that they're not making any headway. Although they spend almost the entire afternoon memorizing Flashcards and looking at problems individually, they don't really feel like anything is clicking. Jake's lack of focus becomes obvious when he starts annoying Bianca by flicking the remaining popcorn bits of their snack at her nose. Soon, an all-out popcorn war has commenced between the two, with all attempts at studying forgotten. Carolina and Nat have the misfortune to enter the dining room at the height of the battle, and flying popcorn fragments bombard them from both sides. Carolina, who spends Tuesday afternoons helping Nat with her class work, shields her face holding her hands up, and hollers over the uproar, "What on earth are you two nuts doing??" The popcorn falls to the floor and Carolina glares at Jake and Bianca, who do their best to hide semi-guilty grins and giggles.

"Bianca, I thought I warned you that Jake is not the best influence. Aren't you guys supposed to be studying?" Carolina asks in a mocking tone. Jake and Bianca start to protest, but Carolina merely stands in innocent silence with one eyebrow raised, and gradually they grudgingly quiet down. Carolina and Nat turn to leave the room, but Jake calls after her, "Hey, wait a sec, maybe you can help us out a little."

Having previously relied on Carolina's proven good advice (and secretly wanting to please Bianca), Jake nags at his sister to help the two of them study for their math and science tests. He shows Carolina the review sheet and the Flashcards that he and Bianca made. With some frustration at having their usual study spot stolen by her sister, Nat dramatically stomps upstairs, huffing loudly that she'll be waiting; it's not like she has any work to finish herself. Meanwhile, Carolina indulges her brother and his study partner, and cranes her neck to see the material. After a few moments of scrutiny, she finally asks, "Jake, do you remember how we studied for your last math unit test?"

"Yeah, kinda."

"Why don't you remind me what exactly we did, for Bianca's benefit of course?"

Jake thinks for a moment, then recites, "Well, first I went through the unit and wrote out all the formulas."

"Ok, and what else did you do?"

"Then I looked through my old homework, and then you made me a practice test to take based on the problems I got wrong from the assignments."

"Right. So . . . why not do the same thing for this test? Create a practice test from the problems that you had any trouble with."

"But there's just so much information. I can't look through every single piece of homework I did. I'll never finish!"

At the same moment, a light bulb goes off in Bianca's head, prompting her to blurt out, "I kept a science Daily Maintenance notebook."

"What does that mean?" Jake asks blankly.

"Well, each day after I finished my homework I recopied any problems that I got wrong from the previous night's homework. I also kept track of any questions that I got wrong on tests. In fact, I did that for both math and science."

"Jake, I hope you know that you seriously lucked out with your study buddy. That's excellent, Bianca!" Carolina chimes in, smiling.

Jake looks regretfully down at his notes, resenting his past decision to mainly overlook Carolina's suggestion to keep his Daily Maintenance notes up to date. While he does have the benefit of having kept track of each individual homework and test, he didn't think to write better running notes of hard questions from each assignment.

"Obviously, Jake, the best thing would've been to refer to your Daily Maintenance work, but at this point, that isn't an option. The next best thing you can do is spend an hour to go over all your old tests, looking at the questions that you got wrong. Then you can look at your homework for extra practice problems and write all those questions into a practice test."

"Got it."

"That is, unless you ask Bianca nicely and she generously decides to share her maintenance notes and compiled practice test with you."

Jake sneers at his sister's back as she goes upstairs to her room, while Bianca grins from behind her maintenance notebook. Jake tiredly begins to pile his science materials in chronological order in front of him, beginning with the oldest material to gather practice test questions. Before he's even made his way through a third of the material, Bianca announces, "All right, mine's done. How about you?" Jake looks up sadly from behind the still-towering stacks of textbook and papers, making Bianca chuckle and say, "Well, I'm kinda tired, so I think I'm gonna head home now. How 'bout we pick up tomorrow with the tests? If you ever finish making yours, that is . . . ."

Jake takes Bianca's sarcasm well, and retorts, "Hah, you're so hilarious. Fine, I'll have mine ready by tomorrow."

"Good," Bianca concludes, satisfied, and packs her things up. "We already know the basics, so tomorrow we can trade tests and see how we do. Oh, and just so you know, I'll probably challenge you to a science version of Trivial Pursuit too, so you might want to prepare yourself for another epic fail on your end." On her way out the door, Bianca flicks a last popcorn kernel at Jake's head.

CHAPTER 11

At the Test—Game On!

All of your practice leads you up to test day. You've spent a lot of time working on learning information, organizing ideas and concepts, and filing everything you know into your brain. The next hurdle is taking the actual test, so now it's time to pull the information out, and get it down on paper to respond to questions. You may think that having all the preparation Tools in your arsenal should make test time a no-brainer but test questions can be tricky, so learning to tackle them is an important step of your study process. No matter how long or short, complicated or straightforward, daunting or easy, follow these steps with each question:

Step 1. Read the question. Slowly and carefully. Twice, if need be. The worst thing that you can do is gloss over a question, grab onto a few key words, and immediately start scribbling away based on what you know about the terms you've fixated on, only to find, when you get your graded paper back, that you've answered the wrong question. You might be surprised at how often this mistake occurs, so prevent yourself from falling into this trap by really taking the time to figure out exactly what you are supposed to explain about the key terms you see.

Step 2. Paraphrase the question. Show yourself that you understand the question. Just because the teacher phrases the question in a particular way doesn't mean you need to use the teacher's words. Saying "I need to answer . . ." is a great way to get your brain to think about each question.

Step 3. Answer before you answer. In the same way that you translated the question from teacher-speak into your own words, answer your version of the question in a way that you best understand it. Jot down a few words, an entire sentence, or perhaps an entire outline. This is especially useful when answering essay questions. Doing this will help you hone in on exactly what you need to cover in your answer.

These steps should help you pace yourself, and work for any type of test question, from those that test your grasp of the basic knowledge (T/F, fill-ins, and multiple choice questions) to your applied understanding of said material (short answer and essays).

What to Do If You're Feeling Overwhelmed

After what seems like countless hours spent studying and preparing for a test, even Mock Test practice cannot completely emulate what being in the actual test is like. It can be as bad as feeling like what skydivers feel: racing heartbeat, weightlessness bordering on fainting, near-physical paralysis, and the vague sense of constantly needing to puke. This is not abnormal, but rather the opposite. To counter these distracting and more distressing sensations, here are a few techniques to help calm your natural reaction to a stressful situation.

We each had a lucky token that we brought into the test and hung onto for dear life throughout it, until we could leave the room and breathe normally again (we carried ours from middle school up through our college years; and have them hidden in a safe spot, just in case). It may sound juvenile, hokey and overly superstitious, but having a physical object gave us comfort, confidence, and even the ability to focus on the task at hand, just by holding it. So, figure out what your own lucky rabbit's foot is, study with it in hand, and take it into tests with you.

Similarly, if you always wore your favorite t-shirt or hat while studying for a given test, make sure you wear it or have it with you when you go into the test. Same deal with using the same pen you took all of your class notes with, wrote out homework in, jotted book notes with, and wrote your test prep notes with during the test. These types of "precautionary measures" are more than just superstitions or voodoo. You've actually become habituated to these objects and associate them with the given material you've been working on. So, remember that necklace you were playing with while reciting the equations for rotational motion, or when you tossed your pen across the room because you were so frustrated with having to memorize the prologue to Shakespeare's *Romeo and Juliet*? These objects can act as memory tools that your brain can associate with the given material you study.

Another step you can take in the actual test situation is when you get the test paper(s), to immediately write down all of the pertinent information that you are most worried about forgetting at the top of a test page. This way you can clear your mind of the worried clutter that mixed in with the information you've studied. Doing this won't get you into trouble, and writing out these facts acts almost as a cheat sheet for the given worrisome facts. By having the concrete reference, you also give yourself the ability to make deeper analyses and Associations, since the facts you're so concerned about are likely to be representative of a larger theme or idea you've studied.

While it too may seem clichéd and "yoga-esque," try to make sure you are taking deep breaths with your feet planted flat on the ground, and sitting up straight in your chair. These physical adjustments actually aid in increasing oxygen flow to the brain, thus maximizing your brain function. In other words, breathing and sitting properly will help your brain not just remember the things you've been stuffing in it, but also allow you to focus on applying what you know and being more targeted in your answers. Similarly, thinking positively about yourself and maintaining self-confidence for a test actually also help your body and brain work to your advantage. This will prevent you from second-guessing your choices in answering questions, and even helps your brain release hormones (happy brain chemicals, like serotonin and epinephrine) that further reinforce your positive feelings about yourself. This translates in real thinking from, "OMG, I'm totally going to fail this test; I can't remember ANYthing I studied!" to, "Dude, I totally killed that multiple choice section." Coming up with a personal mantra you can recite to yourself before going into the test itself can also help amp up your confidence, so be your own cheerleader! This isn't just another stupid suggestion, there's a reason those smiling, perky cheerleaders exist—to get players and fans pumped about a game. It's the same deal with you and the test.

Finally, after all of that work and effort you've invested in the test, (not to mention all of the time you've devoted to studying for the thing), you should leave the test at the test. This may sound redundant, but do just that. Don't get sucked into talking about the test outside the classroom with your friends and classmates. It's entirely unproductive and a waste of time to think about what you might have gotten wrong, not to mention the fact that your friends' answers also might not be correct. In a longer term sense, this will also only reinforce any feelings of anxiety you've got about taking tests, and continuing talk about your possible mistakes only continues the sense of dread you feel on leaving a test, let alone taking it. It's healthier to walk away from a test knowing you did X amount of work studying for it, and you should feel good about having done just that. If necessary, you can even go in thinking to yourself, "I studied so hard for this, I totally deserve the A/A- I'm going to get!"

natalia

After a successful, though somewhat delayed study session with Carolina, Nat walks into her life science class on Wednesday afternoon feeling slightly nervous, but ready to tackle her test. Her lab partner (and friend from drama club) asks her a last minute question about plant structure, which she answers without hesitation, further fueling her confidence. Being overly eager to get started, Nat flips her test face-up without waiting for the entire class to receive copies and scribbles her name and the date on the cover page. She also quickly jots down a few factoids she reviewed at the last minute (including her mnemonic device) at the bottom of the page, before turning to the first questions of the test. She skims the first page of multiple choice questions, and realizes that there are five choices instead of the usual four she's seen previously, and stalls, haltingly reading a choice "E" for each the questions. Nat reads alternately "All of the above" or "None of the above" for each "E" option. She glances up to see that she's not the only test-taker frowning or raising an eyebrow, starts to feel better, and shoots a look at the clock across the room, only to find that she's already spent five minutes worrying about the first page. Nat scrambles to regain her focus and dives into answering the MCs.

After thirty-five minutes and three-and-a-half pages of carefully reading each question twice, underlining key words, and then finally choosing between answers A through E, Nat turns to the short essay section, again pausing briefly when she encounters a short prompt at the top of an otherwise blank sheet of paper. Quickly, Nat skims the question, and is relieved to find that the prompt contains the name for the exact process for which she'd created an Acronym she wrote on the front page, and immediately starts scribbling an answer as quickly as possible. After filling the entire page with every relevant fact she can think of and much cramping in her hand, she sits back to take a brief breather only to be jarringly startled by the grating call of, "All right: you have ten minutes. Start wrapping up," from her teacher. At this alarming news, Nat grabs her pen while scrabbling to turn the page to the last essay. She stares at the question blankly, silently panicking and thus being unable to figure out exactly what the question is asking. Seizing on the words "describe an experiment" at the start of the paragraph, she quickly bullet-points the steps of the scientific method that her teacher has enumerated a dozen times in class. Taking another breath, she returns to the question, and realizes that the topic of investigation is also something she's well versed in: the plant structure she'd just Outlined to her friend before the start of the test. She furiously draws a crude picture of a plant, and scratches some lines directed at near-appropriate areas that she labels. With only two minutes left and wanting to flip through the test one last time, Nat bullet-points more facts she recalls about plant structure and its functions, attempting to jot one point that relates to the scientific method. Now left with less than a minute to review her answers, she quickly turns the pages, stopping short when she has difficulty separating two pages and finds that one is completely blank. Not stopping to think, Nat reads the first question of the page three times without comprehending a single word, and finally gives up and decides to choose answer C. for all questions on that page, resigned and figuring that C must be the answer to at least one of them. She grudgingly hands her test over to her teacher, who has been bleating, "Time's up, let's go," in her ear since she started the skipped page, and sighs heavily as she sits back.

Test Evaluation: So How'd I Do?

While it is important to study, it's essential that studying gets you the right results. Therefore, you must evaluate your study process and, if necessary, make adjustments for the future. Yes, you've already done a great deal of studying, and have reinforced what you've learned, and applied this information and actually taken the test, but you aren't really done until you've reviewed it.

Did You Study Enough?

When you receive a graded test back from your teacher, your first step is definitely not to crumple it up and throw it away. You're not done with it, so make sure to put it someplace you'll be able to find it later, instead of tossing it into your bag where it could become a forgotten mess at the bottom. The next step is to check your grade and decide if you're satisfied with it. If you did well, then you're definitely on the right track with how you studied. But if your first reaction is something like, "Wait a second, that can't be right" or, "WTF," you need to reassess how you've gone about test prep.

If you weren't happy with the results, review the test to see what you did right and what you missed. There are several aspects you need to look at to figure out where you might be able to improve your study habits. First, see if you actually studied the correct material. It is possible to spend a great deal of time reviewing the wrong chapters or units. This is something you typically realize at the time you take the test, but if you didn't figure it out then, double check with your syllabus or your teacher to verify that what you reviewed was actually the stuff you were tested on. If the content tested wasn't in line with what your syllabus or teacher had indicated, you should try to figure out why you were so off the mark. Start from the beginning and figure out where you lost track of your work. There's likely something lacking in how you study, and the best guide to finding that out is your syllabus and

225

homework assignments, especially if you're not so big on taking class or book notes. However, if you were aimed in the right direction in terms of the test content, you may have had issues with how much you studied. Here you really need to be honest with yourself in asking, "Did I really study enough to get the grade I wanted?"

On review of your test, if you find that you mirror Homer Simpson's "D'oh!" reaction (complete with smacking of forehead), then you really didn't study enough, since you clearly remembered (albeit belatedly) the answer but were unable to reproduce it in the moment. Make sure to give yourself sufficient review time in studying for the next test so that you avoid committing "stupid" mistakes. This means that you should review your notes one more time, repeat a set of note cards aloud that extra time before you hit the bed, or rewrite those particularly troublesome factoids that you consistently miss. However, if you find that you not only studied the correct material but knew it backwards and forwards but still didn't do well, the problem lies in how you've studied. Just because you studied certain facts does not necessarily mean you are able to correctly apply them in any given situation. In this case, you should make an effort to expand your study methods to various types. Flashcards are great, but alone they can't cover everything, so you should figure out how to use the data they contain in an essay or switch up the order so that you correlate the facts with overarching themes. In a similar vein, make sure that you've answered the actual question being asked. It's a common mistake to answer only a portion of a question, or even overlook the true meaning of a question (e.g., delete a "not" or "always" from a question). Again, knowing the material here only gets you so far—understanding what is being asked is the key to making sure you get the points you deserve for knowing said material.

How to Improve on Tests

Other things to ask yourself when reviewing your test go beyond knowing rote content. Did you read each question carefully enough, or did you jump straight to answering because you saw a trigger or key word? Did you know the general idea of what the question was asking but have no clue about the details of the topic? In short answer and essay questions, many students often find that the areas they lose the most points in are for grammar mistakes, thoroughness of addressing the question (and all aspects of it), and answering a question thoroughly only to find that the answer given did not match the question asked. Such oversights may seem surprising, but under the high-pressure conditions of the test, being aware of a tendency to make such errors will prompt you to be that much more conscious in reading and answering questions accurately. Such errors can be avoided by practicing in mock test settings and making sure that your ability to maintain focus throughout a given period of time is up to par.

While it may seem like the last thing you'd want to do, one of the best ways to improve your testing skills is to ask for your teacher's feedback. Again, your teacher's goal is to help you to do better and improve your learning and Study Skills, so approach her and seek out more detailed feedback! Getting advice about how you might better approach studying for future tests can not only save you time in figuring out what exactly you did wrong, but also give you new ideas on how you can study more effectively.

Finally, avoid the temptation to ball up the test and toss it into a dark corner of your room. Instead, make note of what questions (both in terms of content and type) you had difficulty with, and file the test away, preferably in your subject binder or folder, so you might refer to it for future exams and as a Daily Maintenance Work source.

natalia

Nat leaves the test feeling somewhat deflated, and has almost a week to recover and nearly forget about her oversights when her teacher hands the graded results back to the class. On walking into the classroom and seeing her teacher moving about the room returning the red-marked papers, Nat hesitantly takes her seat. "Not your best work, Nat," was the comment she receives along with her test, which is headlined by a bright red B- in the upper right corner. Sighing heavily, she starts to flip through the test as her teacher starts the class review of the returned test. She notes with mild pride that the majority of the multiple choice questions (that she'd spent a great deal of time on during the test) remained unblemished by red Xs, surprisingly even on the page she'd guessed C on she sees, relieved at her luck. However, she is greeted by many red notes when turns to the essay pages.

She stares at the first essay, shocked at how much writing her teacher did on the one essay she was actually able to complete. However, she gradually realizes that the majority of notes on the page say the same thing: "not relevant." At the bottom, Nat sees that her teacher only penalized her by a half a point, but included the note "Good to see that you studied hard, but a lot of the information you included is unnecessary and does not answer the question." Somewhat mollified, Nat thumbs to the following page, where she'd bullet-pointed some random facts before running out of time. Her relief at the result of her previous essay's work is replaced with shock, as she sees that she only received three of the possible twelve points that the second essay was worth. In larger writing, her teacher had written the dreaded comment: "See me." Reeling from the massive loss of points on the second essay, Nat is only able to stare blankly at the board for the rest of the class period, and absentmindedly scribbles down some notes when her teacher resumes teaching new material.

At the end of class, Nat's dazed reaction to her essay grade hasn't worn off and she's startled when her teacher calls her over while the class is packing up. Automatically, she snags the test and makes her way to the large desk at the front of the room. "Nat," her teacher begins, finally capturing her attention, "I have a feeling you were pressed for time toward the end of the test." Nodding, Nat quietly hands her test over to the outstretched hand of her teacher, who flips it over to the last page. "I think that you probably studied pretty well for this test, so right now, I'd like you to read the last essay question once more to yourself and take a second to think about it." Nat obliges, silently reading the words in her head, twice just to make sure she's read it correctly, then smacks her forehead, exclaiming, "Oh, come on!" She sheepishly glances at her teacher, who's grinning at her reaction. Clearly, she'd misread the question (if she'd actually read it at all) and answered with something completely irrelevant.

"Exactly," her teacher responds. "I can see that you know exactly what the steps of the scientific method are, but that's not what I was asking about. The question was really about describing an experiment that we'd discussed in class that demonstrates the function of a neuron . . ." ". . . like the frog–electrode experiment," Nat interjects, again receiving another grin in response to her embarrassed apology for interrupting. "Exactly," her teacher repeats. "I can see that you did study and you really knew your stuff, but you need to figure out how to better budget your time when you're taking a test like this. I know the essays are a new type of test question, but they will be a part of my tests from now on and I expect you and the rest of the class to be able to plan out your test time wisely so you can answer these questions properly."

Nat sighs, nodding, and spends another five minutes talking with her teacher about how best to practice and prepare for the essays on future tests before taking off for her next class. After school, Nat bikes through town to the Playhouse, still thinking about the test she made sure to pack in her bag, and about the things she discussed with her teacher. Nat realizes that although she spent a lot of time studying, carefully going through her notes, re-reading the text, and making computer Flashcards, she was nevertheless caught off guard by the test format itself. Giving it some further thought, she decides that just knowing the concepts is really only half the battle and she needs to try to anticipate what types of essay questions the teacher will ask and how best she needs to spend her time in a test setting.

Nat decides that she needs to create Mock Tests with Carolina so she can practice on them, much like her brother and his friend did. Carolina, on hearing this, smiles and suggests that she also use a timer so that she can be more aware of how much time she should spend on each section. Carolina also suggests to Nat that since the essay section was the most challenging for her on the test, she should practice writing full-length essays for the upcoming tests by using the prompts her teacher actually cites in class. Nat had only realized after being told in her meeting with her science teacher that she'd actually known what the essays were going to be on the test she'd just taken. Shaking her head as she kicks her bike into the bike stand, Nat dumps her bag in the auditorium. Since she's taken enough of a beating for the day from her academics, she warmly welcomes her turn to dominate something, and she jumps on stage to join the rest of the cast.

PART V

EMERGENCY PLAN

REMEMBER:
IT'S NEVER TOO LATE!

It always seems impossible until it's done.

—Nelson Mandela

CHAPTER 12

An Eight-Week Plan to Gain Ground If You're Really Stuck

I t's April, or November, or some other month between September and June. You just got back another test with another not-so-great grade, and you realize that you're totally stuck, doing poorly, and have no idea about how to fix the situation. Maybe you've missed handing in too many homework assignments, or forgotten to study for a few too many quizzes. Either way, you're feeling F-ed. Understandably, there are few things worse than the palm-sweating realization that you've messed up, but there are also two important lessons to learn. You can salvage your grades if you put your mind to it and you can learn from your mistakes so that you don't repeat them next year. We get that people fall behind; not everyone can be a Captain America-type student. People make mistakes, and some mistakes are bigger than others. The point here is that we know that things happen, but you should never think it's too late to get back on track. There's always a way to work things out, no matter how dire the circumstances seem in which you might find yourself.

Here's where to start: almost from scratch. You've probably done something in the course of the year, so at least you've got a start point from which you can jump. After scrounging up whatever materials you can, choose a time when you can assess the damage, preferably a longer stretch of time like the weekend, and sooner rather than later. Now is the time to rally your troops (meaning get your act together) before finals hit. What matters is getting back on track, and the only way to do so is if you are truly realistic and honest with yourself about your expectations and how they align with your actual situation.

Week One

First, take a look through your binders, one subject at a time. It's best to start with the subject you're shakiest in, and work on organizing yourself from most to least problematic class. Look at exactly what you do (or don't) have, don't know, or are doing wrong. The best way to do this is to compile all of your tests, review sheets, notes, and relevant materials, and arrange them in designated packets by unit or chapter covered. Don't overstress about getting the paperwork in immaculate order and condition. Just make sure you have what you need, especially all graded assignments (like quizzes and tests).

If your notes are a mess, you will not have the opportunity to get everything in order. Do your best to piece together what notes and handouts you have into a coherent order, but don't pressure yourself to fill in every single hole. You need to stay on top of your homework as best you can, so while the tracking and filing work is important, your top priority should still be keeping up with your most current material.

Week Two

Determine what your specific problem areas or general conceptual difficulties are and create a checklist. For example, figure out if you're doing poorly on your homework, tests, or essays, or recognize that you're not doing work at all for given class X. Make a tentative study plan to give yourself an idea of how much time you have to cover the given amount of material. Be sure to incorporate meetings with your teacher into this schedule to include any extra help time that you may need. Once you've set up a game plan for yourself, don't deviate from it—you've hopefully created a schedule in which you have at least a little wiggle room to adjust your timeframe where needed. Again, you need to make sure that you're keeping up with your current class work, while designating additional study hours for review of older material.

Weeks Three and Four

Now that you've made a workable study schedule for yourself, turn your attention to your actual study habits. Think about how you were studying before, and when you started having difficulty with your class or classes. Usually, you can pinpoint a change in attitude toward a class as a result of a change in study habits and, thus, your subsequent grades produced. If you encountered difficulty comprehending the material at a certain point, as reflected in specific homework, quizzes, or tests, the problem could be either a conceptual factor or perhaps a study approach that isn't right for you. In this situation, don't be afraid to admit that you're having trouble with the material. Go to your teacher or study support for help immediately.

However, if you haven't been studying for a class at all for whatever reason (e.g., you've lost interest in the class or you've been overburdened by personal issues, etc.), you need to figure out exactly where you left off. It's best to start with the most recent assignments (so you don't fall further behind), and work your way back to where you pushed this class work aside. It is tough to try slogging through material you don't enjoy, but do your best. Keep in mind that you only have to do the work for a short period of time. It's helpful to have a study buddy in these situations, so that you can cheer and encourage each other to keep pushing forward.

Weeks Five to Seven

During these last few weeks before your exams, you should be constantly reviewing all the material you'll be tested on, starting with the most challenging, then moving to the easiest. Hopefully, while going through the material, you'll have also made up some study aids to help your review. By now, you should have caught up enough in your backlogged work to do a self-assessment of your grasp of the recovered material. This means going through your homework questions and textbook chapter reviews to make sure you can address all subjects mentioned with relative ease. If there are still concepts that are trouble spots for you, be sure to meet with your teacher (more than once if need be) to take you step by step through the given material so that you identify why your misunderstanding occurred and what the accurate interpretation is.

Week Eight

Make yourself practice tests so you can check up on how good your understanding is of the material and also how your timing is in terms of actually taking the test. Make sure that you aren't trying to cram. Get sleep. Good to go.

jake, bianca, and carolina

Tearing through the school's front doors after his last exam to meet up with his soccer buddies outside, Jake nearly floats with glee at having finished his last exam of the year. The whole team has planned a ceremonial, end-of-the year cleansing bonfire, where they will "sacrifice" the entirety of their lockers. They had initially decided to meet at Jake's house and dump the entire year's contents of their binders, folders, and backpacks into a huge pile, intending to set the whole thing ablaze and perform a victory dance about. However, due mainly to numerous adults' objections, their cleansing ritual has been downsized to tossing everything into a large garbage bag and heaving the thing into a dumpster behind their favorite diner. Joining the guys in pounding on each other and hollering about how thoroughly they'd demolished on their last exams, Jake spots Bianca emerging from the school.

"Hey guys, I'm gonna jet – I'll catch up with you later at the bonfire," Jake yells to his friends over his shoulder, already making his way back to catch up with Bianca, who is patiently listening to Nat enthusiastically narrate how "school is going to be so different next year" for her, since Carolina's been showing her how to study better.

Jake slows as he approaches the siblings, and greets them with a huge grin. "'Sup, Nat?" he crows, high-fiving a giggling Nat. "Hey, B . . . how'd your last test go?"

Bianca's initial reactive smile at Jake's approach dims slightly, and she shrugs, "All right, I guess. I don't really feel like talking about it."

Jake's eyebrows shoot up and he halts abruptly. "Why? You can't possibly be worried about doing badly. It's not like you can jinx yourself. I watched you study 'til you went cross-eyed!"

Ignoring this comment, Bianca frowns skeptically and cocks an eyebrow back at him. "Are you guys seriously doing the bonfire thing?"

Jake hesitates, looking sheepishly over at his friends, who've now started making exaggerated lewd gestures and laughing maniacally in his direction. "Nah, not really. We're just gonna throw away all of our old papers since it's the end of the year. It's not like we're going to need them anymore."

Bianca sniffs, and snobbishly responds, "I see. Well, I like hanging onto my old papers. Especially for subjects that I'm going to continue studying next year, which pretty much translates to all of my classes. I think it's helpful to have them as a reference, just in case."

Jake stares at Bianca in near-disbelief. "But that's so much stuff! And that's just from this year. I'll never go back through ALL that stuff," he says as Bianca's face wrinkles in disapproval and Nat's snickering become more audible, and then hesitantly continues, "I mean, maybe, I might just keep all the finals prep papers that I worked on. I guess that makes sense, since we spent so much time making all of them."

Bianca nods, satisfied. "That's probably a good idea." Bianca has come to realize, after many hours of study sessions together, that Jake tends to take her suggestions with only a little hesitation. Jake, although he won't acknowledge it aloud, appreciates and even grudgingly envies Bianca's meticulous and methodical study habits, and he'd definitely never admit that her suggestions might have been a large part of why he's finished the school year with such strong, satisfying grades.

Just as they start to cross the street, Jake realizes that he has forgotten to empty the remaining dregs of miscellaneous junk from his locker. Mentally kicking himself repeatedly (since this mistake prevents him from following their established routine of his walking her home one last time), Jake groans, "Oh man, I can't believe this. I forgot to finish cleaning out my locker. Sorry, but . . ." Jake stops suddenly, too embarrassed to ask Bianca to wait for him. "Um, well, I guess I'll see you tonight at the dance, then." With the close of the school year, most of Jake's friends had ended up scrambling to find a date to the end-of-school formal. Jake, extremely pleased with himself, was able to gloat about how he'd managed to "win" Bianca as his date, omitting his consequent trouncing by Bianca in later study sessions.

Bianca smiles secretively, and responds airily, "That's cool, I'm supposed to meet up with the soccer girls to get ready anyway . . . but aren't you forgetting about something?"

Jake stares back blankly. Bianca sighs, rolls her eyes upward, and smirks, "Dude. You're supposed to be picking me up so we can actually get to the dance."

Now verging on mortification, Jake hurriedly responds, "Yeah, um, clearly that's what I meant . . . okay, so . . . I'll catch you later!"

Bianca finally laughs along with her infinitely amused sister and turns, shaking her head as Jake takes off back to the school entranceway with a huge, unstoppable grin glued to his reddened cheeks.

Epilogue

If you've read this whole book (or at least skimmed over it), and you're still feeling, "Eh . . . ," that's okay. The amount of information we've included here can seem somewhat overwhelming. It took us a number of years to truly feel comfortable teaching this stuff, let alone use it in our own studies. We were likely only just getting the hang of most of these techniques when we met in Gen Chem Lab I. We don't expect that reading our guide is equivalent to sprinkling magical study powder and we know that it'll take time for all of the suggestions to sink in. Our hope with this book is that you come to think of it as the students we are able to meet with directly do—as something you can turn to if you have any questions about studying or school-related concerns. We want this guide to be an alternative support to our presence in your academic endeavors.

With a little practice, you should find that your studying gets easier, more interesting—and actually *fun*. Thanks for reading—and happy studying!

Index

ABOUT THE AUTHORS

Alexandra Mayzler is the founder and director of Thinking Caps Tutoring (TCT), which develops innovative, individualized approaches to teaching. Mayzler has crafted both a Study Skills program and a series of prep courses for standardized tests, including the ISEE, SHSAT, SAT, ACT, AP, and Regents. She graduated from NYU with a BA in psychology and English literature. She is also a program developer at AbilTo, where she is designing a skills program for college students; she consults with several NY schools regarding curriculum; and is a member of the International Dyslexia Association. She lives in New York City.

Ana McGann is a senior tutor and curriculum advisor with TCT, with which she has collaborated since close to its founding. She graduated from NYU with a BA in Latin American literature and psychology. She has since completed a pre-health post-baccalaureate program and is in the midst of medical school applications. McGann has instructed students in a range of subjects and levels, with particular focus on Study Skills and test prep. She lives in New York City.

Note from the Authors: While we can't work one-on-one with you in person, we offer our continued support in your scholastic pursuits. If ever you want some extra or more individualized input, feel free to contact us at tutors@thinkingcapstutoring.com.